WORK LESS AND GROW RICH

Work ON Your Business, Not IN Your Business

BY

JIM NISSING, J.D.

WORK LESS AND GROW RICH

Work ON Your Business, Not IN Your Business

JIM NISSING, J.D.

ISBN-13: 978-0692740170

ISBN-10: 0692740171

"This publication is designed to provide accurate and authoritative information regarding the subject matter covered. It is sold with the understanding that the publisher is not engaged in rendering legal, accounting, or other professional service. If legal advice or other expert assistance is required, the services of a competent professional person should be sought."

This extract is from a Declaration of Principles jointly adopted by a committee of the American Bar Association and committee of the Publisher's Association.

Laws are ever-changing, and laws vary from state to state. The forms and information included in this book should not be relied upon without consultation with an attorney or an accountant. Because the resolution of a legal issue always depends on the particular circumstances of each situation, the services of a professional in that field should be sought and obtained. Hence, the publisher and author specifically disclaim any personal liability, risk, or loss incurred as a result of the application of any advice or information offered herein, whether directly or indirectly used. Any oral representations made to the contrary of these statements are at this moment specifically disclaimed and should not be relied upon.

TABLE OF CONTENTS

WORK LESS AND GROW RICH

About the Author

Jim Nissing, J.D.

Jim Nissing is the founder and president of the Matrix Financial Network. He has over 35 years of experience as an attorney, financial advisor, strategic planner and coach to entrepreneurs, individuals, and groups.

Mr. Nissing has specialized in corporate law, finance and real estate. Previously he has been president of several companies including a real estate development firm, financial management firm, a hedge fund, and he is an active angel investor for several start-up companies. Jim has been an advisor to the University of Washington, numerous real estate syndications, hedge funds, numerous internet companies, and Global Radiation Environmental Services.

Mr. Nissing has a Juris Doctorate degree from Seattle University School of Law and a BA degree from the University of Washington.

Mr. Nissing is a practicing attorney in the state of Washington practicing law for 35 years with a focus on the legal, financial, and creative aspects of corporate development from start-up through financing and profitable operations. His law firm represents corporations, LLC's, and individuals in their business-related matters, including business entity structuring, seed and primary equity offerings, valuation, incorporation, corporate governance, intellectual property, technology, media, entertainment, contracts, mergers and acquisitions, and ongoing business-related legal advice.

To Alison, Amanda, and Callie

FORWARD

The Matrix described in this book is an extraordinary way of thinking. The Matrix is an intuitive experience which is used throughout this book. It's like tasting an orange. I could tell you a thousand times what an orange tastes like, but until you taste it yourself, you won't know.

I sincerely thank Mr. Sony Suzuki, who introduced me to this experience, 30 years ago.

Sony and I have collaborated for over 30 years, and he is a lifelong friend. We have consulted with many Fortune 500 companies, company executives, and entrepreneurs.

Mr. Suzuki is an advisor and consultant to the government of Japan, IBM and several media and technology companies located in the US, Canada, Japan, Malaysia, and Thailand. Mr. Suzuki has previously held key leadership positions at IBM Corporation as General Manager/Managing Partner and Asia Pacific Practice Leader where he managed IBM's Media and Entertainment sector plus Digital Media Laboratory throughout the Asia Pacific region.

"Happiness depends on upon ourselves."
Aristotle

INTRODUCTION

Why would you want to work less? There can be thousands of reasons. Your family, your kids, your spouse, your friends, golf, skiing, boating, surfing, relationships, volunteering, travel, you name it. How would you like to work less and at the same time grow rich? You think it can't be done. Well, this book is a blueprint on how to do it. I've done it for years. I've learned from the best, and I want to share it with you. You may be working too much, and the rest of your life suffers. Balance is the key. This book will take you on a personal journey, and you will feel more balanced as a result of participating in reading this book and thinking about your life. Well, I've said enough, enjoy your journey.

Why become rich? I'm sure you have lots of ideas and plans about what your life would be if you are rich. Why become an entrepreneur? Freedom could be the first reason. The idea we all want is financial freedom, time freedom, relationship freedom and freedom to choose or find your purpose in life. You want to free yourself so you can experience your most exciting and fulfilling endeavors. We don't want to worry where our next dollar is coming from. We want to be able to do whatever we want when we want. We want to choose our relationships. Always striving for excellence and knowledge and being better than you have ever been before is our goal. We want to find our true purpose in life.

"The journey of a thousand miles begins with one step." Lao Tzu

WHAT IS YOUR PURPOSE IN LIFE?

Have you ever thought about what you were born to do? What do you love to do, what is your passion? What are you naturally good at? What do you want to accomplish in your life? Why? Who is involved? What impact on the world do you want to make? Why? What is your Why? Once you know your purpose, everything falls into place and supports you if your purpose supports others. Purposes change over the course of a lifetime but think about your life.

Do you work all day and at the end of the day do not feel satisfied? Was it a waste of your time? Or at the end of the day are you satisfied that you created something and expressed yourself. You need to figure out what is the purpose in your life. Assess where you are now and where you want to go and how to get there.

This also applies to business. What is the purpose of your business? Why? Are you helping others? Do you make their lives better? Do you have customers or clients? The customer is a one-time sale. A client is someone you are committed to making their life better. You look out for the best solution for your client whether it's your product or service or someone else's. Figure the value of a lifetime client to you. This is someone you are protecting, and they come back for your products or services for years and make referrals.

Remember your best experiences in business. Maybe you've been fortunate to have many businesses. Think about the good times and the bad times. Visualize your favorite business and see yourself being extremely successful at it. See the rewards from your efforts. Feel the elation of doing what you enjoy doing. Say you'll never give up. Always build on your successes.

I have clients that ask me how to become successful or how to solve a specific problem. I always ask them what is their purpose in the situation or their purpose in life. This is very important because some people know where they are but have difficulty in knowing where they want to go. Some people do not know where they are and do not know where they want to go. First, you need to know where you are right now. Asking what your purpose in life is will be a starting point. Then you can think about where you want to go.

Also, I ask them the same question that I will ask you: Let's say we were talking three years from now and you were looking over those three years. What has to have taken place in your life, both to your career and to you personally, for you to feel happy with your progress? Think about this. What has to have happened for you to feel happy with your progress?

Also, what threats you must overcome, what do you need to optimize in your behavior, and what opportunities do you need to go with. You need to apply SWOT to your purpose. SWOT stands for strengths, weaknesses, opportunities, and threats. What are the strengths, weaknesses, opportunities and threats to your purpose or your business?

Many times when clients come to my office, I find that they didn't have a goal or purpose. A driving purpose is essential for success and organizing your affairs. If you don't know where you are going, you won't know what to pack for the trip. This book for those just starting out and for established entrepreneurs to focus on their purpose and realize that purpose. This book will give you techniques to define your purpose in life and then how to stay on course. A purpose is a journey and not a destination. Also, success is a journey and not a destination.

After you are aware of your purpose then you can create a business, which operates even when you are not around. Can you leave your business for a week, a month? 6 months? That's the ultimate when your business is working for you and you are concentrating on what makes you happy in your business and in your personal life.

These are exciting times. Small businesses, companies with fewer than 500 employees, employ over 70% of the work force. The real economic news these days is being made in thousands of home offices, small office parks and garage factories around the country. With the internet, and computers, our home offices are as efficient as large downtown offices and we are freed from commuting. In fact, exurbs (extra urban) are already becoming a trend. An exurb is a community located 100 miles from a city where community values flourish, where you know your neighbor, and you have a safe place for your children to grow up. You do your business on the internet with your computer. You don't need to commute.

This book is for you even if you work for someone else. Large corporations are forced to be entrepreneurs because of rapidly changing markets and times. They must adjust to compete, so must you! These corporations are restructuring their organizations to utilize the Entrepreneur spirit and creativity for new products and markets. Then they will use their established leadership skills to market the product.

If you do not want to own your own company, this book can assist you in creating a new position within a company of your choice. In today's economy large employers often are not hiring, so you need to create a new position for the company. Visualize yourself as a company president and see where the company needs to go to survive in today's market. Then solve the company problem by showing them how you can take them where they need to go.

Everything in relativity goes through three stages: creation, preservation, and change. Your body goes through all these three stages – Firstly you are born (created), Secondly you struggle for your living (preserve) and then you leave for the heavenly abode (change) but spiritually you will never die. When you plan your estate plan, you see that many years are devoted to creating your estate, then you preserve it, then you pass it to your family, friends, and charities. Leave a legacy.

Business goes through the same cycles. Some believe that corporations never die, but look closer. Corporations are tied to their customers or clients, to product lines, services and their acceptability to consumers. They must change with the times to survive, compete with themselves, with new products and new markets. Any change in clients, products or marketing signals an end of a cycle.

A product group will crest then fall, the best companies continue to research new products and markets and that is why they continue. They listen to their consumers. People create trends and companies sell what those people want. The intent of the corporate structure is to allow the business to perpetuate indefinitely, the assumption is that it will stay current with the market. Look at the failure of even whole industries because of the change in markets or competition. Many record pressing plants went bankrupt because they didn't get into compact discs. Now CD companies must find a way to make downloads profitable.

The only constant in business is change. Know your market changes, know the perceptions of your buyers and know the image you are presenting. When you get comfortable with your business success don't stay comfortable too long, keep up with the latest trends. Be disruptive in the market place.

How much lasting happiness will we find if we start a business and then it fails? Perhaps some happiness can be found for the creative effort but we want lasting success, so we must ensure that we move to the preservation stage with proper leadership techniques. Then at the end of the cycle we will decide where our creation is to end up.

Being an entrepreneur is one of the most exciting and satisfying experiences in life. You are in total control of your business and you chart your course in life.

This book is a process which will focus you on your purpose for your business and your life. Your purpose is focused and you are committed and that's why you will succeed, but you will need tools to hit your target.

The key in business is to love your clients and look out for their best interests. There is a difference between you customers and you clients. Customers are a onetime sale. A client is someone that trusts you and your company and they will buy from you again and again and refer you to their friends. Figure the value of a lifetime client and you will see they are the life of your business.

Some say starting a business is risky. The only risk is giving up, quitting. When you are committed to your purpose you know you will never give up. Don’t allow negative thoughts from others to deter you. Find someone, a friend or mentor to support your cause. Pound the rock. You keep beating that rock until it cracks. You may not even chip it for a long time. But keep hitting it harder each time. And after repeated beatings it suddenly cracks in pieces. You are a success. Success doesn't happen overnight. When you are committed to innovation and committed to making a difference, you will persevere. When you are committed to serving your clients best interest you will succeed. Hire people who know more than you do. Bring in the best experts. Learn from their advice. You will learn about the master mind later in the course. Be consistent in your leadership. Develop loyalty with everyone in your company or business. Set an example. So many people plant a seed and want to see the plant the next day. Know that the seed is growing. Water it, nurture it. Know that you will see the plant. It's up to you to set the example.

Too many people use failure as a label, for themselves. Failure doesn't exist for you. Do you know why? The reason is you are not a 'failure' if you have learned something from that situation!

Information technology has changed our economy. Computers, software and the internet give small business the same access to information that until now only large businesses could afford. Now you can start a company at home and compete with companies that have been in existence for 50 years. You are able to add value in niche markets and you were the only one who saw the need. You can market one to one on the internet. You may find others have the same needs and expand your business. You could start a trend, or supply a trend that no one else saw.

Our economy changed from a managerial society to an entrepreneur society. No other country in the world has experienced this yet. We want to make a difference. We want to create, do our part and be unique. We have the freedom for uniqueness and the commitment to make it work. We're confident in ourselves, and of the route we have taken. The tests that life takes will shake us in short term, but we move on towards maturity and greater understanding. With greater understanding we hone our skills until we can create. We create in search of excellence. It's the satisfaction, the process, the thrill no one can take away from us, or give to us. We have created something unique. And the end is only a new beginning, because we feel our creativeness in the process of change. New beginnings are 'Growth' and this new beginning i.e. growth is preserved and managed well, until we begin again. The end, or profit or completeness is only a point of change.

The thrill of accomplishment inspires us. We don't hold on to our accomplishments, we give them up, and find even greater rewards in our gift. We keep score with our happiness, our freedom our purpose and how many clients we have helped. Money is a vehicle to create, to fulfill our purpose. Our purpose drives us, money is like a car, sometimes it's shiny, new and works, other times it needs repair, but always we are the one driving it. Know where you want to go and go.

The Matrix Financial Network is dedicated to entrepreneurs and investors. This is a network of opportunity. Our business model gives an opportunity not only to the investors who are looking for an investment or business but also to those property owners who are looking for investors. Let us know of your success. Our website will highlight your success story and the opportunity you have engineered. It is a forum for investors and entrepreneurs. It is an opportunity to mastermind with other investors.

We can show you where the doors of success are, but you are the one who must open the doors of your life. Be open to success. Know that failure is only a learning process. Learn to fail your way to success.

When you find your inner wealth you can attract outer wealth. Without inner wealth, outer wealth is meaningless. But, is that really true? If I have a new car, a bigger house, then I'm wealthy, am I not? If I have... then I am. No, that's not true. If I am... then I have.

If you are inwardly a beggar, then outwardly you will be a beggar. When you have to have this, and have to have that to be this then you are a beggar! If you are inwardly wealthy, then outwardly you will be wealthy. Wealth begins with you. Are you wealthy? Go inward and see. Are you happy? Are you fulfilled? Are you healthy, are you peaceful? Is your life rich with friends and family? Are you suited for your career? Do you enjoy your work? Do you know your purpose in life? Use happiness instead of dollars to evaluate your success.

To find your purpose in life a good exercise is to find out what areas you are outstanding. Take out some paper and a pen and write down what you do every day for a week. Use a calendar and just note what you do every hour of every day for a week. This gives you a vision of yourself. Then at the end of the week look for trends. List all of the activities where you were outstanding. Next list the activities where you were skilled and refined but didn't necessarily have a passion for it. Next list the activities that you were able to complete but again you didn't have a passion for them. Next list the activities that you were not good at and that you didn't want to complete. Now you want to brainstorm on how you can improve or increase the areas that you are outstanding. Also you want to find ways to delegate the other areas or manage the areas that you are skilled. Look to delegate the areas that you are not good at.

Then write down the description of your outstanding areas and your skilled areas and the competent and not good areas. Condense your thoughts to what you are really outstanding and why you are outstanding.

Once you are successful and enjoy your success you become comfortable. The irony is that becoming comfortable could limit your success. In the next chapter we will explore the Comfort Zone.

"The greater danger for most of us lies not in setting our aim too high and falling short; but in setting our aim too low, and achieving our mark." Michelangelo

COMFORT ZONE

What happens when you are earning enough to be comfortable? Yes, you are comfortable. Your business maintains your lifestyle. That's cool. But if you want to grow your business so it is saleable then you will need to get outside your comfort zone. You need innovation to grow. You have success and now you need to interrupt your success and try something new. Not a new business a new way of expanding. You can expand through new hires, partnerships and joint ventures.

Look at Maslow's hierarchy of needs.

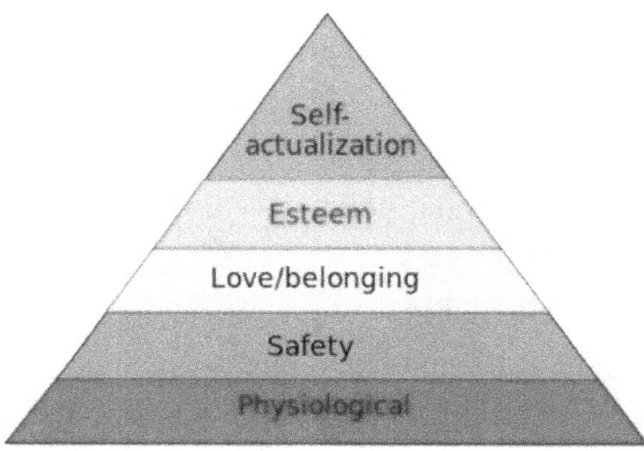

Maslow's hierarchy of needs, represented as a pyramid with the more basic needs at the bottom.

Maslow's hierarchy of needs is a theory in psychology proposed by Abraham Maslow in his 1943 paper "A Theory of Human Motivation" in *Psychological Review*.[2]

Maslow suggests that the most basic level of needs must be met before the individual will strongly desire the secondary or higher level needs. People must be motivated to go beyond the scope of the basic needs and strive for constant improvement. Ultimately, you want self- actualization.

This is the trap of the Comfort Zone. When we achieve a satisfying level we are comfortable and are not as motivated to continue to improve.

Many courses begin with a course outline and books to read and then you get a test to see how much you have memorized, or how well you can logically manipulate the information. You learned how to do that in elementary school, high school, college and graduate schools. Many people call this left brain thinking.

Generally, public education and colleges do not teach right brain thinking. Right brain thinking opens your creative self, your artistic self, your humanity.

The synthesis of left and right brain thinking into will power will direct you to fulfill your purpose in life.

Science says that most of us use only a fraction of our brains functioning ability. Even Albert Einstein said he used only fraction of his brains functioning ability. So instead of force feeding our active logical mind more of the same, this is an opportunity to utilize the rest of your mind and access your hidden capabilities.

Remember: Commitment to your life is the key.

Each one of you has decided to read this book for a reason. Only you know the reason or reasons you've chosen this book. This material is designed to work with reasoning so that the reasoning of your life will become your will power. Your will power will transform your life. Your expression of life will be unique. You will have the identity of 'Your Own'!

Many of us think we are expressing our uniqueness but often we are rearranging our comfort zone. The comfort zone can be described like a living room. We see nice furniture, a TV set, wine, ice cream, popcorn, good food, beer, fireplace and plants. Once we establish this zone we feel comfortable being there. We are not challenged. We are identified with the thoughts and objects in the zone. This is the 5 percent of the brain that we are familiar with, actually even less than that because research shows that sometimes up to 90% of our thoughts are negative. Assuming negative thoughts are not comfortable that leaves us with 1 or 2 percent of the brain in the comfort zone. This is not real inspiring. It's no wonder that we want to continually rearrange the comfort zone to make it appear different and contemporary because we get bored with it.

We buy new cars, clothes, furniture and we accumulate more things in our zone - computers, phones, boats, cameras, and games. And mentally we process more and more complex thoughts but we process the thoughts in the same way. We are playing the same tapes in our mind that we have played for years. Our mental comfort zone is full of comfortable ideas; ones we have known for years. These are the thoughts that we believe, and these beliefs form a mental cocoon. Then we feel uncomfortable venturing out of the cocoon. We add many logical connections to our core beliefs. We rearrange our ideas to give us the feeling of progression. But for real progression and personal growth we need to utilize more of our brains functioning ability.

The problem with comfort zones is that they become boundaries rather than sources of inspiration. These boundaries become our identities. We work so hard at our self-identity. We want to look a certain way and we want to be a certain way. This course is designed as an opportunity to observe your own identity – yourself and to discover your real self-image. Your real self-image is where the source of great inspiration lies.

We all know how to think, analyze, rationalize and create identities. There is something else we can all do. Be aware. Can you tell whether you had a sound sleep in night? We are aware when we are asleep. We are even aware when we analyze and rationalize. When we don't want to be aware we can attempt to shut off our awareness by flooding our senses with food, stimulants, and depressants. However, it is difficult to shut down awareness completely since we can always remember the state that we were in. Awareness is one of the keys to success and to satisfaction in your life.

When you taste an orange, can you describe the taste to someone else? You can try but soon you will realize that there is no way to transmit your experience of tasting the orange to someone else. They have to experience it themselves. In the same manner this book must be experienced. If I tell you about it, all I can say are generalizations, and ideas. To experience this book you will experience your awareness.

Check out the Matrix Planner in the next chapter. The Matrix Planner can unlock some hidden passions you have and find ways for you to act on them.

"We are what we repeatedly do. Excellence, then, is not an act, but a habit". Aristotle

USE THE MATRIX PLANNER TO WORK LESS AND GROW RICH

Success begins with you. You are in control of your life. Your decisions bring about the results in your life. Your spiritual actions cause the spiritual results in your life. Your mental actions cause the mental results in your life. Your material action causes the material results in your life. Life is simple. You are the architect of your dreams and your actions in life determine your results in life.

Be concerned with who you are not what you have. In life as well as in business you need to know who you are. Know what your values are and know what results you will get from your values. Reflect on your values and if there are some you don't like, change them. Be aware. Be honest with yourself, because if you know who you are, you can see others as they are. Then you will be able to form lasting and satisfying relationships with others.

Ask yourself, what is my purpose in life? Once you know your purpose in life you can you can reflect your purpose in life into your business. Then your business will have you and your purpose behind it. Then you will succeed as never before. You will grow as a person and your business will grow to benefit others.

You must look within to find the purpose in your life. The MATRIX PLANNER is designed to assist you in focusing on your purpose in life. The next section is the MATRIX PLANNER commitment section. Spend some time going through the exercises. Use the contracts in the planner to fulfill your commitments in your life. Make your life unique. Do something no one else has done.

Balance in your life makes you happier. How many outwardly wealthy people do you know who are unhappy, leading empty lives? Moreover, how many unhappy people do you know? Money will not make them happy. Happiness comes from living a fulfilling life. What makes a fulfilling life? The balance of friends, family, satisfying work, helping others, spiritual life, mental challenges, a healthy body, financial success, and organization makes life fulfilling. I recommend that in the beginning you fill out the six basic contracts: Contracts on your SPIRITUAL LIFE, your MENTAL LIFE, your BODY, your RELATIONSHIPS, your FINANCIAL LIFE, and ORGANIZING YOUR LIFE. Of course you may have other contracts you wish to write.

The Matrix Charts are very important. They help you focus directly on your purpose, they are a quick reference, and they are a dynamic tool in which to chart your course to success. To get a yearly Matrix Planner go to *MatrixFinancialNetwork.com* to order one. The following pages are out of the MATRIX PLANNER. Use your MATRIX PLANNER every day. Keep notes in it. Notice 'Who' are you? Notice what you are becoming. Notice with whom you hang out with! Use the MATRIX PLANNER to focus on your commitments. Every day make your purpose in life, a reality. Try to make progress in each of your commitments!

MATRIX PLANNER

FOCUSING ON YOUR COMMITMENTS

SUCCESS DIAGRAM

WRITE YOUR NAME IN THE FIRST CIRCLE

WRITE UP TO 7 AREAS YOU HAVE EXCELLED AT ANYTIME IN YOUR LIFE IN THE SECOND CIRCLE

WRITE UP TO 7 AREAS THAT ARE IMPORTANT TO YOU AT ANY TIME IN YOUR LIFE AND THAT YOU CANNOT LIVE WITHOUT IN THE THIRD CIRCLE

WRITE ADDITIONAL AREAS YOU ARE GOOD AT IN THE FOURTH CIRCLE

USE NOTATIONS IF YOU DON'T HAVE ENOUGH SPACE OR USE LARGER CIRCLES

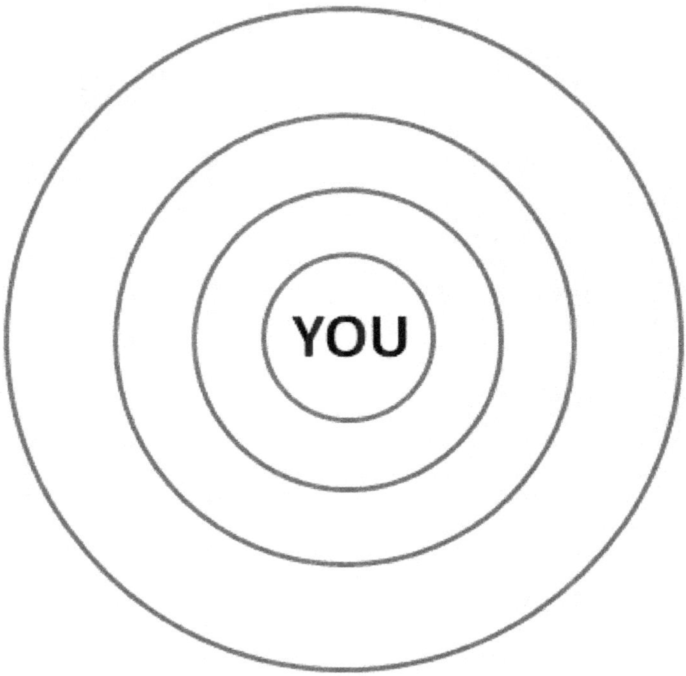

YOUR COMMITMENTS

WRITE CONTRACTS ON SPIRITUAL LIFE, YOUR MENTAL LIFE, YOUR BODY, YOUR RELATIONSHIPS, YOUR ORGANIZATION, YOUR FINANCES, YOUR 90 DAY PLAN, ONE YEAR PLAN, AND YOUR THREE YEAR PLAN. THEN WRITE ALL OTHER CONTRACTS YOU WANT TO!

FIRST STATE WHAT YOU ARE COMMITTED TO IN LIFE?

SECOND WRITE WHY THE COMMITMENT IS IMPORTANT TO YOU.

THIRD WRITE HOW YOU WILL ACCOMPLISH YOUR COMMITMENT. DO YOU NEED TO LEARN SOMETHING NEW? WHAT TYPE OF EXPERTS DO YOU NEED TO CONSULT WITH? WHO IS ON YOUR SUPPORT TEAM?

FOURTH WRITE THE DATE YOU WILL ACHIEVE YOUR COMMITMENT.

FIFTH WRITE HOW IT FEELS, LOOKS, SOUNDS, TASTES, AND SMELLS TO ACCOMPLISH THIS COMMITMENT? VISUALIZE YOURSELF ACCOMPLISHING THIS COMMITMENT.

YOUR COMMITMENTS

CHART YOUR COMMITMENT STATEMENTS ON A CIRCLE CHART. WRITE YOUR NAME IN THE FIRST CIRCLE, AND WRITE UP TO 7 COMMITMENTS IN THE SECOND CIRCLE, AND YOUR OTHER COMMITMENTS IN THE THIRD CIRCLE.

REVIEW THESE CHARTS AS OFTEN AS YOU FEEL NECESSARY BECAUSE YOU ARE CHARTING THE COURSE OF YOUR LIFE!

AFTER YOU CREATE A CHART OF ALL OF YOUR COMMITMENTS, WRITE A STATEMENT OF YOUR PURPOSE.

WRITE HOW AND WHEN YOU WILL ACHIEVE YOUR PURPOSE.

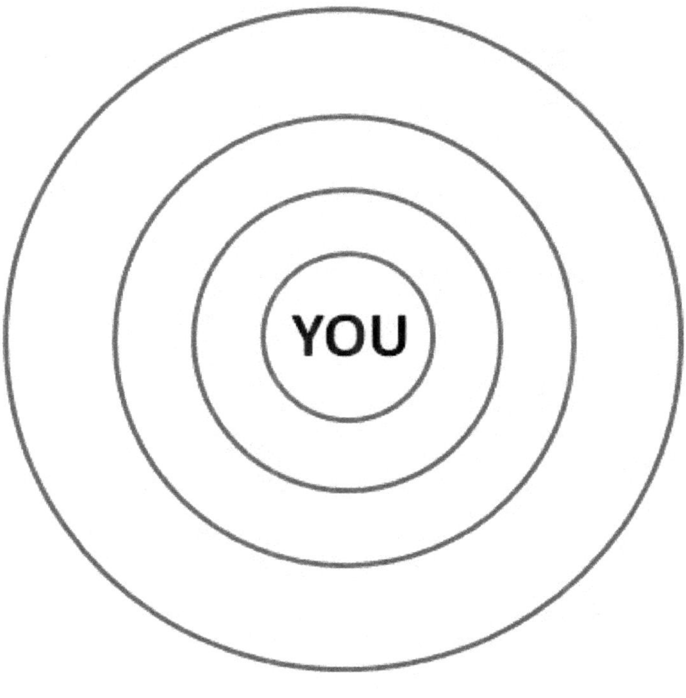

YOUR COMMITMENTS

USE A CIRCLE CHART FOR EACH COMMITMENT. PUT THE COMMITMENT IN THE FIRST CIRCLE AND THEN UP TO 7 DETAILS IN THE SECOND CIRCLE. PUT THE BALANCE OF THE DETAILS IN THE THIRD CIRCLE, AND YOUR RESISTENCES AND FEARS IN THE FOURTH CIRCLE.

REVIEW THESE CHARTS AS OFTEN AS YOU FEEL NECESSARY BECAUSE YOU ARE CHARTING THE COURSE OF YOUR LIFE!

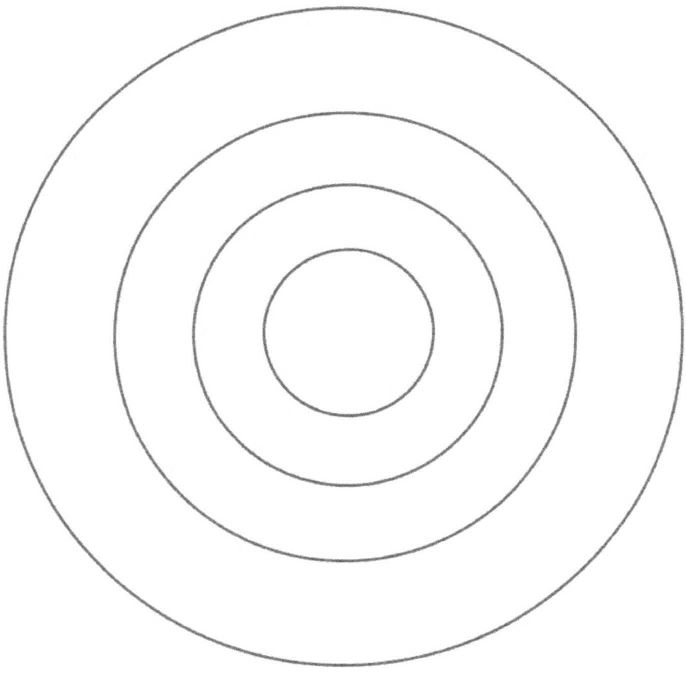

The following are examples of charting each commitment, starting with the whole picture and then exploring each commitment.

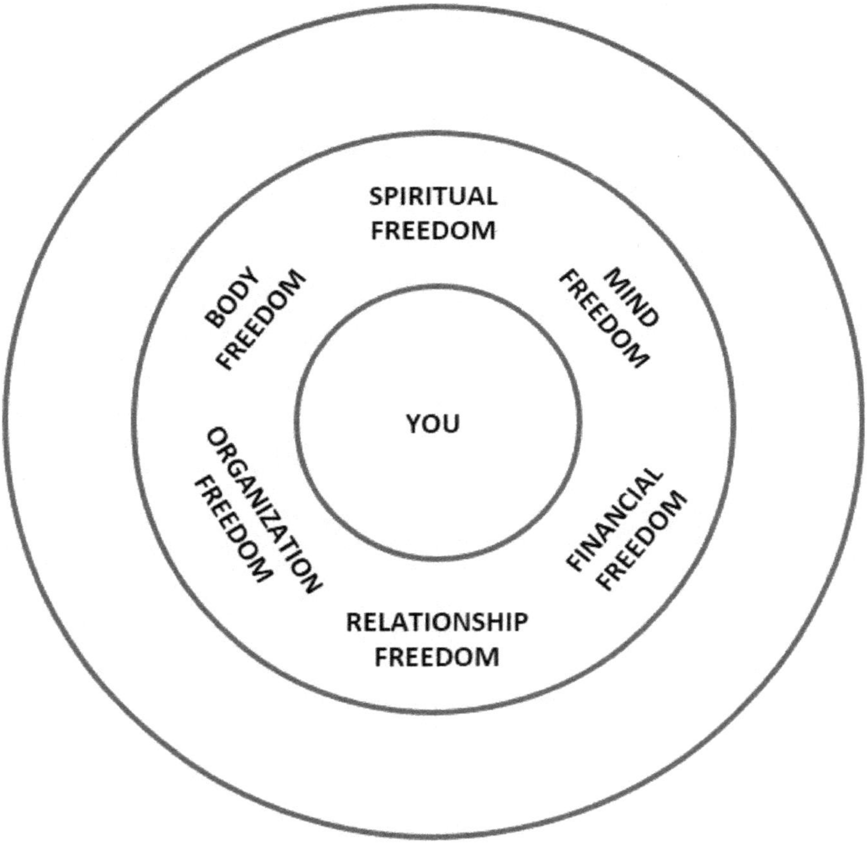
SPIRITUAL FREEDOM
BODY FREEDOM
MIND FREEDOM
YOU
ORGANIZATION FREEDOM
FINANCIAL FREEDOM
RELATIONSHIP FREEDOM

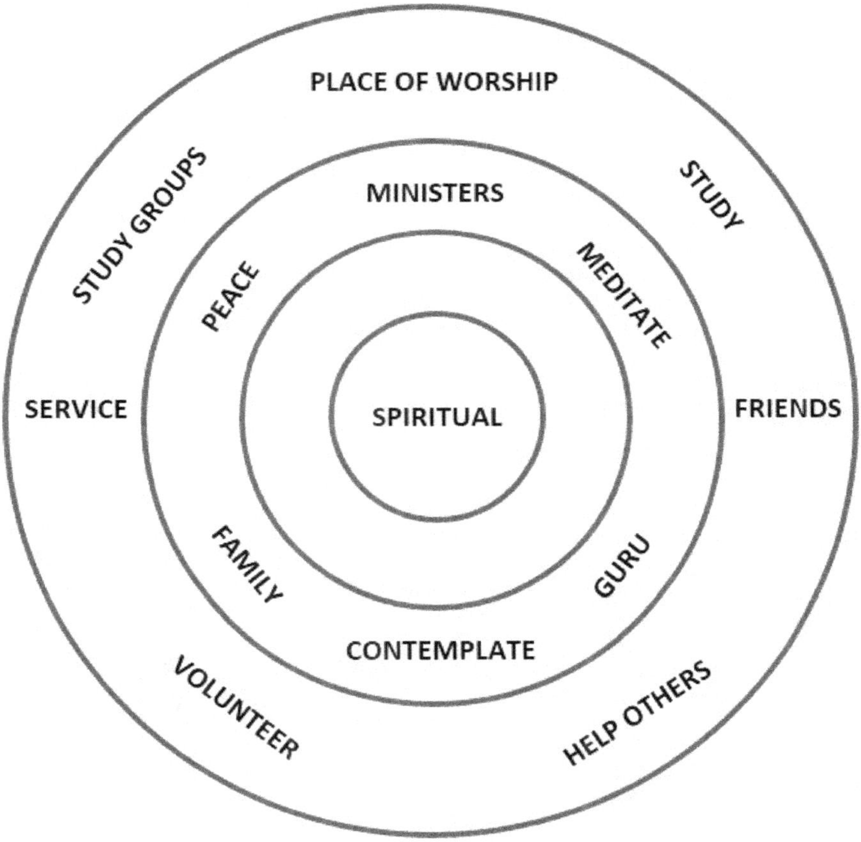
PLACE OF WORSHIP
STUDY GROUPS
STUDY
MINISTERS
PEACE
MEDITATE
SERVICE
SPIRITUAL
FRIENDS
FAMILY
GURU
CONTEMPLATE
VOLUNTEER
HELP OTHERS

SEMINARS, WEBINARS
MASTERMIND
RELATIONSHIP FREEDOM
INSPIRE OTHERS
FINANCIAL FREEDOM
MIND
PURPOSE
TIME TO DO WHAT WE WANT
MATRIX
HELP OTHERS TO BECOME SUCCESSFUL
STUDY

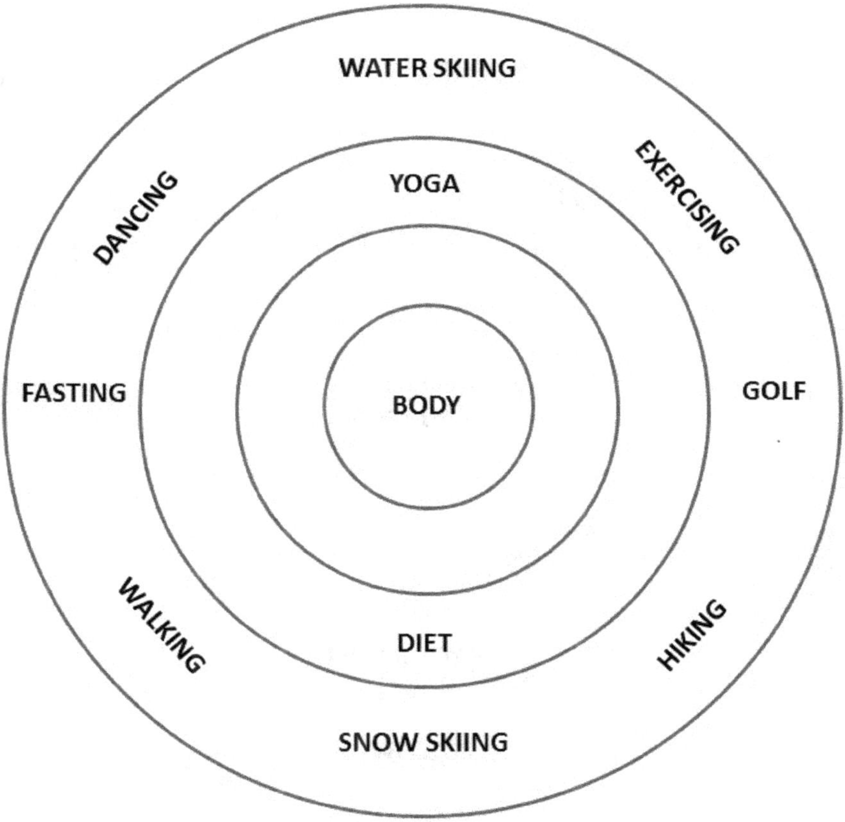
WATER SKIING
DANCING
YOGA
EXERCISING
FASTING
BODY
GOLF
WALKING
DIET
HIKING
SNOW SKIING

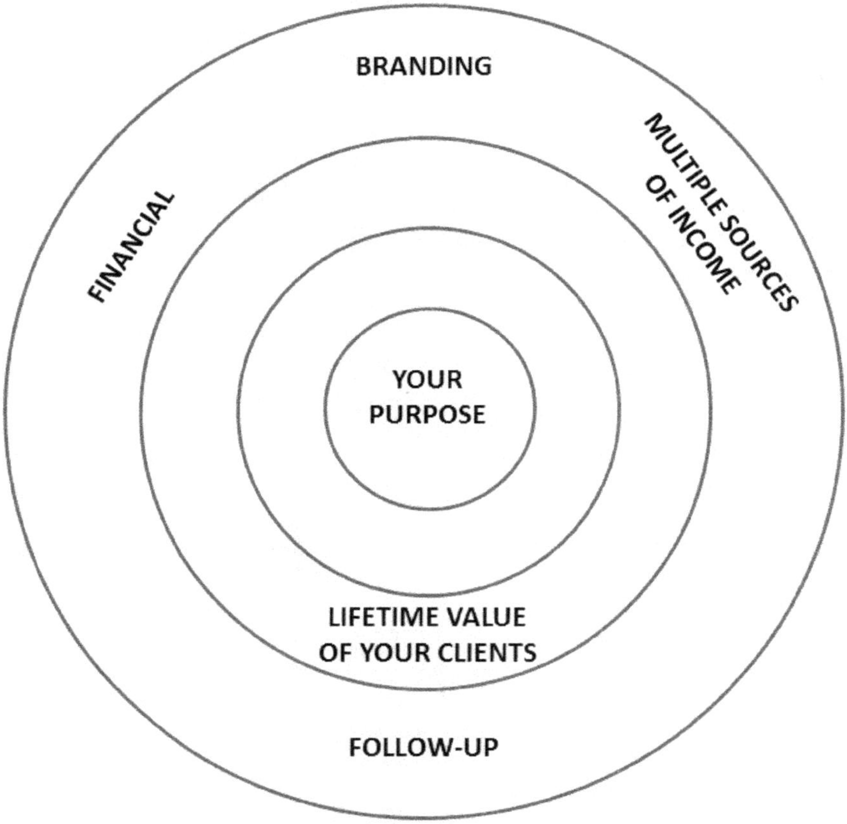
BRANDING
FINANCIAL
MULTIPLE SOURCES OF INCOME
YOUR PURPOSE
LIFETIME VALUE OF YOUR CLIENTS
FOLLOW-UP

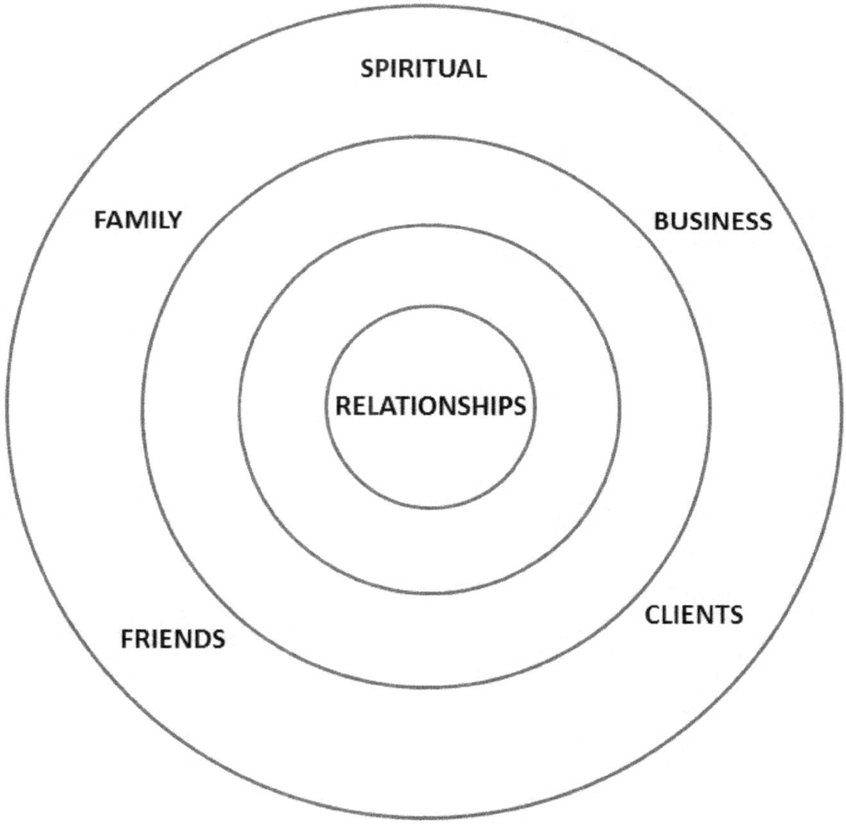
SPIRITUAL
FAMILY
BUSINESS
RELATIONSHIPS
CLIENTS
FRIENDS

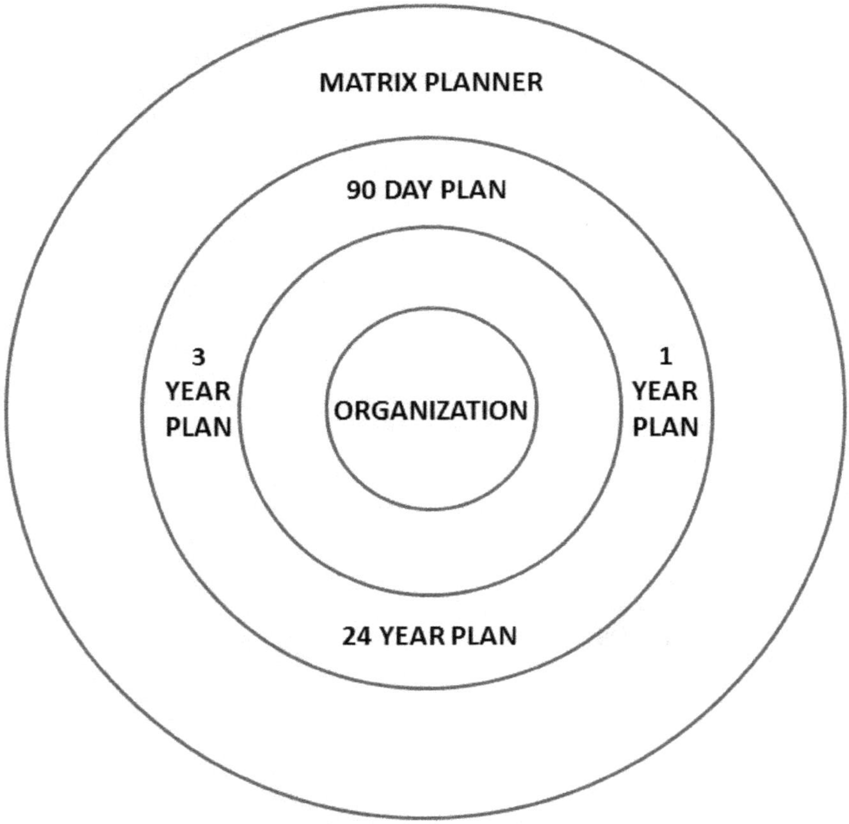
MATRIX PLANNER
90 DAY PLAN
3 YEAR PLAN
ORGANIZATION
1 YEAR PLAN
24 YEAR PLAN

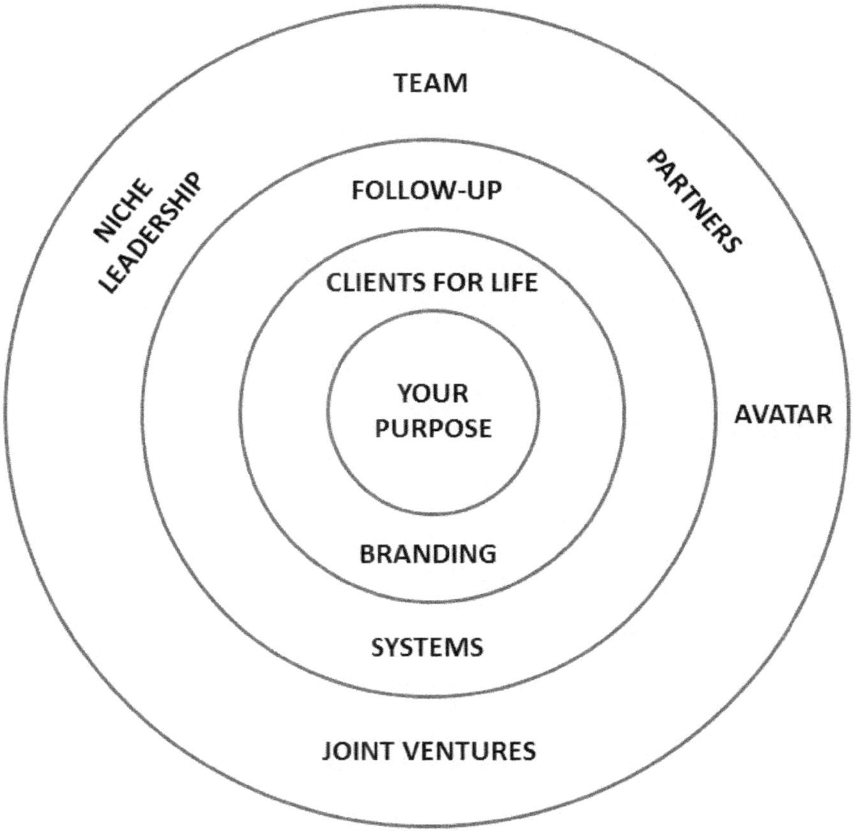
TEAM
NICHE
LEADERSHIP
PARTNERS
FOLLOW-UP
CLIENTS FOR LIFE
YOUR
PURPOSE
AVATAR
BRANDING
SYSTEMS
JOINT VENTURES

You can apply each one of your commitments to each project or each business that you own for extreme efficiency.

MATRIX: MULTIPLE SOURCES OF INCOME

BUSINESS 1 BUSINESS 2 BUSINESS 3

MATRIX: MULTIPLE SOURCES OF INCOME

BUSINESS 1 BUSINESS 2 BUSINESS 3

REALIZATION

COMMITMENT PHOTOS

FIND OR TAKE PHOTOS WHICH REPRESENT FULLFILLMENT OF EACH OF YOUR COMMITMENTS.

SPIRITUAL

MIND

BODY

RELATIONSHIPS

ORGANIZATION

FINANCIAL

ENTREPRENEURS

USE A MATRIX CHART AND PUT ALL OF YOUR DIFFERENT STREAMS OF INCOME ON THE CHART WITH THE PRIMARY ONE IN THE CENTER.

"Time is a created thing. To say 'I don't have time,' is like saying, 'I don't want to." Lao Tzu

MATRIX PLANNER

The MATRIX PLANNER is organized to focus on your commitments. Begin by focusing on 6 commitments: Spiritual, Mind, Body, Relationships, Organization, and Financial commitments. Every day when you are scheduling time and people, review your 6 commitments and make sure they are on the schedule.

We suggest that in the morning take some Spiritual Time for an hour. Focus your attention inward. This is the time to use any meditation and contemplative techniques you know. Then look forward at the day. Visualize yourself being successful in the day. See your appointments and projects resulting in success.

Next spend some time Organizing. Review your commitments, and update your charts of success. Then, write down what you are avoiding. Accomplish these things first. Then write the 20% of the most important things for you to do. Many time management courses state the 20/80 RULE. 20% of your activities will account for 80% of the results in your life. So concentrate on the 20% of the most important activities in your life. Then write the remaining 80% of your activities. Since these activities will account for only 20% of your results, delegate as many of these activities as you can, or transfer them to another day. The key in procrastination is to procrastinate all of your unimportant activities, (often they will vanish), and always do your most important activities first.

Next develop your Mind. Write the discoveries and breakthroughs you make every day. Also write dreams you remember. Save your Planners, and over the years you will see your growth, and have a record of it. Spend time reading, develop expertise, and cultivate your interests.

Find time for your Body. Spend time every day exercising. Use the circle charts to focus on what type of exercise interests you. You may spend 5 minutes or an hour; the key is to find something interesting. Learn about your diet. Chart your course. Choose healthy things to eat. Find time to relax. Look for deep relaxation through music, reading, and meditation.

You should schedule time for your Relationships. Use the Matrix circle charts to learn about the people you care about, and those who care about you. Also use the circle charts for important and unimportant business relationships. Look for opportunities to share with others, and to teach others.

Schedule your Financial Activities. Use the Matrix circle charts to focus on your objectives and commitments.

One of the keys to building your wealth in business or real estate is to be aware of your efforts. Monitor your efforts and increase your business and real estate awareness. On DEALS EVALUATED write the number of opportunities or properties you evaluated that day. Evaluating a business or a property doesn't necessarily mean that you physically inspected it. It can mean that you reviewed the data on the business or property. Next, write the number of OFFERS MADE that day. Then write the number of Deals Closed that day. The Total Amount is the total dollar amount of deals closed that day. The Month Total is the total dollar amount of deals closed that month. Also summarize each month's total of opportunities or properties viewed, offers made, and deals closed.

When your active day closes or before you go to sleep, find time to calm yourself, to be contemplative and meditative. Also spend some time looking back on your activities of the day. If there was something that didn't go the way you would have liked, change the picture in your mind to be the way you wanted it to be.

Congratulations for those of you that thought about the six most important areas of your life. As you know there is always resistance to you plans. Sometimes it is other people who resist your plans, sometimes it is you! The next chapter will help you break through resistance.

0	0	0	0	0	0	0
M	T	W	Th	F	S	Sun

MATRIX PLANNER

People
Spiritual
Clam inner focus
Look Forward

Organization
Review Commitments
Complete activates you are avoiding now.
20/80 in action

Mind
Write purpose, discoveries
Breakthroughs, dreams
Read

Body
Exercise
Diet
Relaxation

Relationships
Circle Charts
Sharing
Teaching

Financial Activity
Review Circle Charts

Spiritual
Calm inner focus
Look back

6:00
7:00
8:00
15
30
45
9:00
15
30
45
10:00
15
30
45
11:00
15
30
45
12:00
30
1:00
15
30
45
2:00
15
30
45
3:00
15
30
45
4:00
15
30
45
5:00
30
6:00
7:00
8:00
9:00

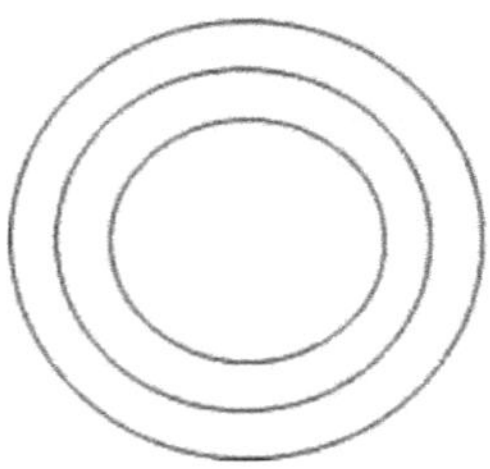

Top 20%

80% Follow Through

Finished √
Delegate D
Tomorrow →

NOTES

EXPENSES

	Offers Made
	Deals Closed
	Total Amount
	Month Total

"At the center of your being you have the answer; you know who you are and you know what you want." Lao Tzu

WORK ON YOUR BUSINESS NOT IN YOUR BUSINESS

Life planning is about designing your plan and then implementing your plan. To make your plan successful you will need information and experts, but information and experts are easily obtainable. Implementing your plan is often difficult because you are moving beyond where you were before. You are stretching your comfort zone, and subconsciously you may have a lot of resistance to change, because you are comfortable. This is why you hear of people who become successful and then all of a sudden lose everything. Why? Some people sabotage themselves. They deliberate harm themselves to get back to where they believe they should be and that is their "comfortable" comfort zone. Most often comfort zones are more limiting and stifling than comfortable. Why? Comfort zones are formed through habit. Bad habits and good habits establish fortified comfort zones. Whatever we learn as conditioned behavior we find comfortable.

It's like the elephant being tied to the little stake which holds him there. How can a little stake hold the elephant? Because when the elephant was little it was tied to a similar stake that he couldn't move and now the elephant retains his childhood belief.

POSITIVE - NEGATIVE

Take two pieces of paper and place one on each side of a table. To your right, write down on the top of the paper: the positive habits, activities and beliefs of my life. On the paper on the left side of the table you are going to write down, the negative habits, activities and beliefs of my life.

Now it is time for you to state both categories. Take your time; write down each item very carefully. Again, you are the only person who can break this chain so we alert you to be as aware as possible. Carefully analyze your behavior, physical habits, language, and diet. Do not miss anything. After you are finished, meditate on these papers. Surprised? If you are not, we suggest you reconsider your process and repeat it again. Now it is time for you to transfer negative habit activities and beliefs to the positive side using a new sheet of paper. Determine each thought, discriminate the reason these thoughts have evolved in you.

You will find some of these thoughts to be very old, and you will also find some of these thoughts and habits to be very recently acquired.

You will find yourself solving uncharacteristic thoughts and habits and finding the reasoning behind them.

Now it is time to make a contract. Take another piece of paper and write a contract stating your name, date, goals, and the date that you will accomplish these goals by. It is important for you to write down a precise plan to accomplish these goals. Attach your contract to the other two pieces of paper and file it. Repeat this exercise once a month. If you feel it a necessity or urgency in your life, repeat this exercise as often as once a week!

VALUES AND BELIEFS

Write up to 7 commitments and values. Then write what feeling you get from that value.

Write up to 7 values and feelings you want to avoid.

Write 7 beliefs which support your values.

Write 7 beliefs which do not support your values.

Change or amend any rules you need to, to accomplish your values.

Pick a negative belief or association that you want to change, and imagine your-self say 5, 10 or 15 years into the future. With that belief, what you will be doing, how will you look? Now come back in today's situation - it didn't happen, and you can change it! Change your posture, talk and energize yourself. Now see a positive manifestation and see yourself 5 10 15 years into the future. Now make your choice of what you are committed to. Write your new commitment in your planner. Take 10 minutes to rewrite your commitment and your statement of your purpose in life.

What holds us back – Fear? Fear of the known, fear of the unknown. Fear of failure, fear of success. We have learned fear; fear is conditioned from experiences. One of the best ways to overcome fear is the following exercise. You literally erase the fear that holds you back, yet you as mature person realize that some activities will harm you and you need to avoid. Some fear is good, common sense is good. Some fear cripples you. Unlearn this fear. Give yourself permission to be free from that fear.

Remember a difficult situation in your life, one that gives you Fear! Now relax and take a deep breath. Give advice to your past and notice those factors on what you were reacting to. What was your intention? What judgments have you formulated? Now imagine yourself in a beautiful theater - A comfortable theater, with plush chairs. Relax. Take a deep breath. Now imagine yourself in the projection booth. You will be running the pictures of your life. First run the picture forwards in black and white. Then imagine yourself up on screen and jump into the picture and run it in color backwards. Run the films several times forward and backward. Use common sense not to put yourself in real danger, learn about what you are afraid of, and keep the part that protects you. Then run the film fast speed forward and backward. You can even play comedy music as you run your films. Smile. Now imagine yourself in the circumstances that you were afraid of. What is the reaction? If you are still afraid then run the films again.

ARE YOU STUCK?

If you have a behavior which controls you or you are stuck and can't seem to move on, consider breaking the loop or interrupting the story. You need to look within at what is bothering you. Be aware of your self-talk. Is it negative, positive, lethargic, funny? Think about what's most important to you at this time or related to the problem. Have a dialogue between what's holding you back and where you want to go. Interrupt the old loop or pattern or story. Think of a really pleasant time in your life, feel it, relive it, stay there. Visualize your new life without what's holding you back. Now relate this change to your purpose in life.

FAILURE

Failure is the judgment! Let's use our ability to judge and redefine failure. If you learn anything from a situation, then it isn't failure. Since we always learn from our experiences failure doesn't exist. Learn what you can from a situation and then forget it. It's like a bad golf shot. Can you learn anything from it? If the answer is 'yes' it is fine but if the answer is 'no' then also it is fine! Then forget it and go on to the next shot with a clear mind.

LIFE CHART

Try the following exercise. Write down your date of birth, then leave space and write down a date 100 years in the future. Write down the highlights and lowlights in your life. Then connect the points. Ask yourself out of which experience you learned the most from. Often a setback is the stimulus for great success later on. The most successful people have learned to "fail their way to success".

Pick one of the experiences that you were not happy with. Imagine a still frame of the scene. Then begin reducing that scene to a smaller and smaller size until it disappears. Just as soon as it disappears see a new scene gradually emerging. This scene is a picture of exactly how you would have liked the original scene to have turned out. Swish these scenes 5 or more times. Every time the old scene appears swish it to the more desirable scene.

SUCCESS

Let's say you want to be successful. Alright! Now, remember what you felt at any successful time in your life. Happy, empowered, grateful, peaceful, fulfilled. Great! Now, begin your new endeavor with that feeling and stay focused and let that feeling manifest into what's important for you. If you get off course go back and remember your successful times and begin again.

The following exercise is about your connection with others.

In the center circle place your name in it. This is you. Think of people who you feel the closest to, people who you think know who you really are. People who love you is for 'who' you are and not for 'what you are! Place their names within the circle on the circle line. Write down no more than seven names in the second circle.

Add a short statement under each name describing why they love you and also very carefully write down the reason you love them.

On the second line from the center, write down the names of fourteen people who you think of as friends or merely as a nice people. These are the people who you contact in your life frequently for business and personal life. These are the people who like you for what you put out to them as an energy exchange in your relationships. Do not exceed fourteen people and repeat the same process as in the first circle, which is: write down the name and then write down what they like you for. Underneath the line write down what type of positive energy exchange you maintain with this person.

On the third circle, it is time for you to place the individuals you know as acquaintances. Do not exceed twenty-one people. Write down these names on the line of the third circle. By now your paper may be getting crowded so you might like to use numbers to keep track of people. Again write the name down; underneath the name what they expect from you. Carefully examine their expectations about you, the reason the expectations exist.

In the last circle write down the names of those people who you consider difficult people to deal with! Write down the reason your emotion exists. Write down their demand on you, underneath.

Now, it is time for you to relax. Be completely free of the process. The next step is: Blank your mind and drop all preexisting notions, feelings, emotions, and judgments about all the individuals who exist in chart.

Start from the outer circle. Carefully meditate upon each individual and the image you have and then, move steadily towards the inner circle. When you finish, close your eyes and try to observe all your relationships and judgments of relationships. Please keep in your mind that you are a witness.

Now go to the center of the circle again and bring one hundred percent of your mental concentration. Bring your whole ability of mind and try to see you as the image from the point of view of every person who is on the chart. In other words, try to see their image of you through this chart.

This process can be applied to your company. If you deal with many organizations, simply replace the names of individuals with the names of organizations.

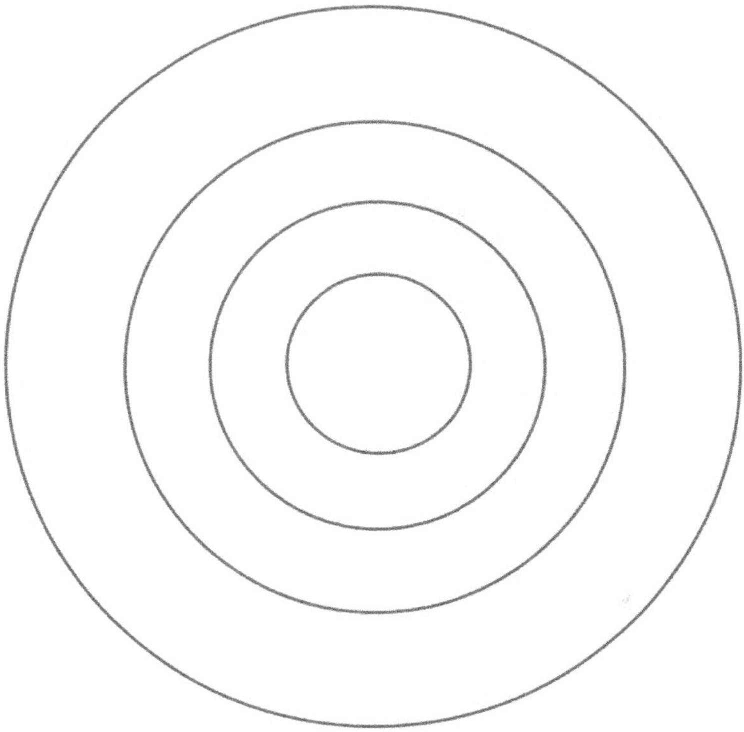

MARRIAGE

The best couple's advice is that when one spouse starts talking, all you need to say is "tell me more". Don't judge. Listen. Don't judge after you have heard it. Encourage the other person.

Now that you have found ways to move on, the next chapter will outline a blue print for success: where you can work less and grow rich!

"By three methods we may learn wisdom: First, by reflection, which is noblest; Second, by imitation, which is easiest; and third by experience, which is the bitterest" Confucius

REALIZATION PRINCIPLES

The **REALIZATION PRINCIPLES** are principles which are designed to refine your focus in life and give you new inspiration for your activities. Generations of successful people have used these principles.

BE AWARE. Be aware all the time of what you are doing. Awareness allows you to always see who you are. When your awareness is acute your memory will be accurate. It's important to see the pictures of your life. You will want to review them to see where you are going. Also you will want to create pictures of where you are going.

BE HONEST. It is the only way you will know who you are. Truth and honesty will radiate from you, and you will attract people and resources to fulfill your purpose. Dishonest people forget who they are. They start believing their own lies, and then they cannot even keep their lies straight. They lose touch with what is real. You need to know what is real for success.

BE OPEN FOR SUCCESS. Being willing to be successful may be a new way of being for you. It's risky doing something new, but it gets less and less risky when success becomes a habit and when your confidence level rises. Start with little things first to build your confidence and then continue to challenge yourself with bigger projects.

DEVELOP YOUR INTUITION. Napoleon Hill in "Think and Grow Rich" called intuition the sixth sense, and all of the wealthy people of his time had it. Know when you are right about something. Allow your conscience to guide you. Meditate before you make a decision. Let your awareness give you feedback on your intuition.

DEVELOP YOUR COMMITMENT. Think about your successes, and what you are good at. It could be organizing, playing, caring for other people, sports, or business-- look within and you will find it. That's your winning attitude. Become informed, think and meditate on your purpose and when you know it's right for you, jump in with both feet. Use the MATRIX PLANNER to focus on your commitments.

DEVELOP DYNAMIC WILLPOWER. Allow your realizations and awareness to fuel your commitments. Tap into the inexhaustible inner source of wealth. Meditate on your Spirit. Let this inexhaustible energy flow through you. You are excited about life. Your enthusiasm reflects who you are. Exercise your willpower. Start with something you can succeed in, and then expand your willpower and your mission in life. Do something great which no one else has done.

TURN YOUR FAILURES INTO SUCCESS. Determination makes the difference between success and so-called failure. Learn to **FAIL YOUR WAY TO SUCCESS**. Learn from your failures, and then let them go. They are like bad dreams. They are not real, they are learning experiences, and they are your stepping stones to success. Accumulate your energies expended in reliving failures and fuel your commitments. Failures are lessons, for success. Once you learn the lesson, drop the experience like a bad dream. There is no purpose in reliving failure unless you haven't learned the lesson from it. Success can be relived all of the time. Visualize your success. Don't believe in other people's negativity. They believe in their own negativity, that's why they know nothing will work. They have proven it for themselves! When others are being negative toward you or your purpose, always be aware that they are speaking about their lives not yours. They are projecting their doubt on you. Just observe. It is them. You are someone else. Your inner realization isn't in them it's in you. Project your inner realization and enthusiasm to them and inspire them. You will be surprised. Watch your thoughts. Are they positive or negative? Get into the habit of thinking positive thoughts. Positive thoughts will attract success.

BE FOCUSED ON YOUR COMMITMENTS. Dale Carnegie said "Put all your eggs in one basket, and watch the basket." Don't diversify. Specialize. Be a success in one area. Only after you have obtained confident success, are you able to diversify. If you diversify, be sure to diversify only into related areas. Don't be like the large corporations which buy unrelated subsidiaries, only to sell them at a loss a few years later, because they didn't know their clients, products, markets, or specialty. Do not spread yourself so thin that you do not concentrate on your commitment. Focus on your target. Hit your target. Get the knowledge necessary. Use your MASTER MIND GROUP, for needed expertise. Develop your own expertise, so you know what a good deal is. After you have been making it and have some successes don't get side-tracked. You will have all kinds of offers of "GREAT" deals, unrelated to what you know. All those "GREAT" deals just take time and energy away from your purpose. Don't dilute your energy. There are many people who will want a piece of your success because they are too lazy to be successful themselves.

USE YOUR MASTER MIND GROUP. A Master Mind Group is a group of people who assist you with their expertise. The master mind allows your mind, and expertise to expand. You will be able to make the most complex decisions and be right. Your planning and expertise will be on target to your purpose in life. Always use the best experts available. The cost to hire the best is very little more than the cost to hire mediocre "experts," and in the long run the cost will be less because of the superior advice you will receive. The best experts will benefit you deeply, and make you more money. Don't try to be an expert in every area. If you need additional expertise find an expert to fill the gap. Meet with your group often, individually, and as a group.

JOIN A MATRIX MASTER MIND GROUP. A Matrix Master Mind Group has meeting with a small number of members. They discuss their successes and problem areas. They discuss solutions and directions. The group holds them accountable to make improvements and be successful. The group supports you to be successful.

SPECIALIZE. Become a specialist in an area you choose. Go to seminars, read, and take courses in your area of expertise. Help yourself to keep your knowledge growing. Be able to be successful when circumstances change. The world is ever changing. As an expert be able to see the changes and, be creative in your response to change.

NEVER GIVE UP. You may not see results right away. When you plant a seed you cannot expect it to grow if you dig it up every day. Water it, nurture it, and love it. The seed is you. Stay on purpose; make decisions every day that keep you on purpose. Your commitment is real. Determination is success. Don't stop digging your gold mine when you are only 6 inches away from the richest vein.

ORGANIZE. Knowledge is power. NO! Napoleon Hill said knowledge plus organization and direction is power. Use your

MATRIX PLANNER to focus your energy and knowledge on your purpose.

BE GENEROUS! Give some of your wealth away to those who need it--charities, causes, Spiritual organizations, and friends. Give some of your inner wealth as well as your material wealth. It is a never ending cycle, you receive your inner wealth freely and you give freely. Think of all the joy when you receive something. You will receive all of that joy and more, when you give the same thing away.

BE HEALTHY! Breathe deeply. Deep breaths calm the body and clear the mind. Exercise is essential. Your body is your vehicle. Do keep it rolling and fit. You will feel better. Keep your spine straight. Not because finishing school demands it, but because energy flows up and down your spine, and when it's bent the energy is blocked. That same energy makes you money and makes you wise. Maintain a good diet. Eat when you are hungry. If you put good things into your body you get good energy from them. Cut down on white flour, sugar, glutens and meat. See what happens.

DON'T WORRY-- BE HAPPY. Live without fear. Know that when you have found your mission in life others will help. Become happier every day. Keep a list with you as to why you are happy. Measure your success with happiness.

Use the **REALIZATION PRINCIPLES** every day. Be happy. Balance your financial life and family life. Have time for spiritual and mental pursuits. Be in good shape and fulfill your purpose in life.

THE REALIZATION PRINCIPLES work for personal growth, for any type of business, and they work for large organizations. For the entrepreneur they are invaluable. Visualize being at the controls of your jet plane ready for takeoff and you have a complete working knowledge of the airplane and know how to fly. You are exhilarated and ready for takeoff. You get your clearance and taxi down the runway, accelerate, and soar into the air, headed for your favorite destination. That's what it is like, using the realization principles.

Use the **MATRIX PLANNER** to increase your productivity. Now you will be able to plan your vacations and family time in much better way! Learn to do the things that you want to avoid first. The things that you avoid are challenges in your life. Look forward to moving on to new heights. The Planner is simple to use and clarifies this complex world. The Planner allows you to focus on the 20% of activities in your life which account for 80% of the results in your life. The planner sets you free of the 80% of activities that account for only 20% of results in your life by delegating them or procrastinating.

PROCRASTINATING. You've probably heard that procrastinating is a terrible thing to do. Actually it is one of the keys to success. The key is to procrastinate doing the secondary 80% of the activities that account for only 20% of your results. Do the things that you are avoiding first, your day is then a success. Next, do the most important 20% of your activities after you accomplish what you were trying to avoid. Most time-management courses emphasize the 20/80 rule. The MATRIX PLANNER puts the rule into action and you benefit from it.

This book shows you how to create a balanced business. Also we show you how to balance long term holdings with short term investments, and we show you techniques in managing your cash flow with multiple profit centers. There is no question but that it is important to blend liquid investments with long term growth investments. Also insurance and estate planning are a part of the balance formula. But before we chart our course for greater wealth, let's ask "Will your business set you free or will your business be another job?"

JIM NISSING, J.D.

"Strive not to be a success, but rather to be of value." Albert Einstein

WILL YOUR BUSINESS SET YOU FREE OR WILL YOUR BUSINESS BE ANOTHER JOB?

The key to success is to ask yourself, why do you want to be in business? Your answer to 'why' is a driving force behind you! Do you want freedom? How about financial freedom? How about the freedom to choose your purpose in life? How about the freedom to choose your religion? What about the freedom to choose your relationships? How about freedom to concentrate on your unique strengths?

If you are able to optimize your unique strengths and delegate you will create a business where you do not have to be present 24/7. Otherwise, as often the case a person creates a business and it is a job. A job that requires you to be there round the clock!

The greatest risk in business today is not doing anything. If your salary does not keep pace with inflation, then your earning power is diminished every year. You can't get ahead. Your dollars buy less and less each year. Owning your own business is one of the best investments, because you leverage your time and skills.

Traditional stock and mutual oriented retirement plans are subject to market corrections like we saw in 2000. However, self-directed retirement plans, including Roth IRA's and Roth 401K's allow you to invest in hard assets and businesses. Discounted mortgages and real estate purchased at the right time can outperform the market and offer more stability.

Social Security isn't a safe bet any longer for substantial retirement income. In ten years who knows what the status of Social Security will be? How about next year? We have seen hundreds of Savings and Loan institutions close. Security lies in an investment which is stable, which keeps pace with inflation, and is profitable. Your Stability lies in your ability to analyze change in your business and its markets, then to be able to organize your response to that change.

Why invest in your business? If you have a cause or a purpose and can express it in business, then you will make a difference to other people. You will make this world a better place. You will always be successful when you alleviate other people's miseries. Challenge and stretch yourself to do something no one else has done. You help others through win-win negotiations, and you help your clients, employees, and customers.

The energy you put into a business organization has value. Also the markets you develop and your client lists have value. If you buy a business below market you have a profit going in. You could sell the business the next day and make money. If your business concept is good and your business is sound you can sell stock to the public, with the help of your attorney. The successful companies that have gone public have yielded enormous profits to their founders. Bill Gates became one of the wealthiest people in the world by creating a successful company, Microsoft, and taking it public.

When you own your business you are in control of your future. Millionaires realize the dream that they designed. You no longer run the risk of layoffs, dead end jobs, superiors who don't appreciate your work. Your health is at risk if you don't enjoy your work. You minimize business risks when you become an expert in your field, stay focused and respond and learn from change. Do successful people measure their success with dollars? No.

Successful people measure their success with the realization that they have helped others, that they have fulfilled their purpose, and with the realization of being happy and healthy.

Millionaires put other people's wealth to work for their cause. Other people's wealth includes time, services, money, financial statements, other assets, experience, energy and lender's money. One of the keys in business is to leverage your time and resources. One of your most valuable resources is the people in your company. They allow you to multiply your efforts. Hire people who know more than you do. Then delegate to them to free your time for your next step.

The key to leverage is that the return on your investment is based on the efforts of others. If you work hourly, you have 40 to 50 hours you can work in a week. If you own a company with 100 people you now work 4,000 to 5,000 hours per week. That's leverage.

Another way to maximize your leverage is to borrow the money it takes to buy a business or the equipment you need.

Cash flow is what you want out of your business. The trick is to keep your invested cash as low as possible and in reserve, and build your cash flow from your business. Managing cash flow is essential. It happens too often where someone has a great concept but runs out of cash to market the concept. Plan your cash flow as much as you plan your concept that you are marketing.

Your percentage of interest in a business is how much you own of the business. You want to protect your interest or investment. You want to legally control your business because you are responsible and others may not be.

Partnerships are bad news. Even if you are the controlling partner often there are circumstances beyond your control. If your partner gets sued and gets a judgment against him or her for say

$500,000 that judgment would end up as a lien on his or her interest of the partnership. You may end up with a new partner, or not be able to make decisions with the consent of your partner's creditor!

In corporations, control is always an issue. Always maintain a controlling interest in your company. It's like the old story where two owners with 50% shareholdings each, gave one share of stock to their secretary. Then one owner runs off to Las Vegas with the secretary and they have a board meeting and vote out the other owner from an active position!

You may not have all the expertise or funding you need to run your business and to attract the expertise and capital you need you need to give up an equity interest. Use royalty agreements where the contributing person gets a percentage of profit and you keep legal control. This is utilizing the spirit of a partnership without the risk of partnership.

Develop your business to the level where you could leave for a month or two and it would still be there when you got back.

There are other models for business. If you have a cause or purpose that you share with others then look into a nonprofit corporation or NGO, non-governmental entity. There are no shares in the company and the board of directors controls the company. Should the company break up, all the assets must be donated to another nonprofit corporation. There may be many federal, state, and foundation grants available to the nonprofit corporation.

Owning your business is the best tax shelter today. You can expand your business with "ordinary and necessary" business expenses which offset your income. You will be able to depreciate your equipment and property which will offer additional tax shelter. You can elect to pay yourself a salary or a dividend from the corporation which will change the amount of tax you pay. Since tax laws change every year, be sure to have an accountant or

CPA in your MASTER MIND GROUP to advise you on your next strategy.

You will want a strategic plan to work 'On' your business not 'In' your business. The plan is to set you free. You want to plan your business so you don't have to be there to run it. Then you will have a saleable business. The next chapter explores elements of strategic planning.

"Because one believes in oneself, one doesn't try to convince others. Because one is content with oneself, one doesn't need others' approval. Because one accepts oneself, the whole world accepts him or her." Lao Tzu

STRATEGIC PLANNING

Divide your business success plan into three functions: Define your Purpose, design your Life Plan, and do Matrix Strategic Planning.

DEFINE YOUR PURPOSE

As an innovator, look for something simple, easy to understand and think small. Visualize your product or service working at an individual level, one to one. You want to dominate a small niche of clients. Then look for growth opportunities, and larger markets. Don't look into the future too far; create something that can be used now. Then make your first steps. For many people the curtain never goes up.

Build on your strengths. Create something new in an area in which you are an expert. Don't jump to a new area of creation because most likely you will just be learning the basics.

When you analyze a business opportunity, analyze the deal, the economic figures, the product, the clients and the people as well! Who is involved? What is your gut reaction to them? Do you want to work with them? If your gut reaction is to get away from them then do it. Get away! I've seen deals where the product was good and had a lot of potential but the people that were involved were dishonest. There is no way you will make a deal work when you are dealing with dishonest people.

Focus on your clients. Describe your perfect client. Give him/her a proper name! List all of their attributes. This is your market. Design your marketing campaign to attract this client.

DESIGN YOUR LIFE PLAN

Define your purpose and then design a precise life plan to fulfill that purpose. A life plan may include a business plan for the financial aspect of fulfilling your purpose in life. A business plan is a set of blueprints for the business. It shows in detail where you are now and where you are going. Whether you are building a new business or buying an existing one you need a business plan.

Be specific. In business you need a definite date and specific dollar amount for achievement. Successful owners review the plan often. Let the plan grow with your company. Write it down and update it in writing.

MATRIX STRATEGIC PLANNING

You need a detailed roadmap to design your company. Start with your business plan and keep updating the plan. The exercises in this book will give you a good start. As you grow you can bring in the same type of expertise that is used by larger companies. Your business plan can be the basis for a Private Placement Memorandum (PPM). With a PPM you can attract accredited investors, qualify them and advertise for them under Reg D 506C. Also you can make a crowd funding presentation. You will need a securities lawyer to guide you through the process and to be compliant with the rules.

"Stop thinking, and end your problems."
Lao Tzu

BUSINESS STRATEGIC PLAN

OPTIMIZE YOUR EXISTING SOURCE OF INCOME

ADD MULITPLE SOURCES OF INCOME

BUILD YOUR CLIENT LIST AND NETWORKING

USE THE MATRIX FINANCIAL NETWORK

OPTIMIZE YOUR EXISTING SOURCE OF INCOME

As you focus on your unique individual talents you need to look around and see where you are. You need a realistic view of what your business or income stream is all about. What makes it work? What are your obstacles? What opportunities do you have? What is the role where you excel? Look at your branding and marketing. After you observe your business you need to optimize it so it performs the way you want. If it isn't what you want, take note of your individual talents and look elsewhere.

MULTIPLE SOURCES OF INCOME

Having multiple sources of income is a plan of security. If you have one piston in your engine and it stops, you stop. If you have eight pistons running and one of the pistons stop then the others will keep you going. Someone who makes money in a business or a job needs to invest it. You need your money working for you.

Look for investments related to your core business. For instance, real estate investors can look into buying discounted mortgages, or hedge funds that specialize in discounted mortgages. Become knowledgeable in what you put your money into, and don't diversify too much. Stay focused. Too much diversity can dilute the focus of your investment. Optimize and upgrade your existing business before you venture into other sources of income.

SUCCESS NETWORKING

I know, this sounds like one of those events where everyone hands out one of their cards, and tells you two seconds of info about what they do and then it's your turn. That's random networking, somewhat like a dating service. Collecting business cards is useless unless you follow up can call them back. It's better to meet a few people who you have rapport with and can discuss your business opportunities.

Networking needs to be strategic. You need to pick the people in your network. Use the master mind circle chart to identify the people, professionals and marketing people you need in your network. Make your cause known to people. Trust your intuition in networking, you may not be able to use a certain connection now, but a time will come when that connection will fit perfectly. Have your elevator pitch ready to go when you meet people

You need people who will expand your network so that it will benefit your purpose. These are those people who can expand your network by linking you with other strategic networks. License other people's email lists to promote your business. Share the return. Get endorsements, they are introductions to their network. Concentrate on excellent people in your network, then each one of those people will refer you and advocate of your purpose. They also become a representative of your purpose to the networks in which they belong. This becomes an enormous expansion of your network, almost overnight.

MATRIX FINANCIAL NETWORK

The Matrix Financial Network supports you to dream your dreams and realize your dreams. You can join this network for social and business connections which will last a lifetime. I've seen too many organizations which are helpful for a while and encourage someone but later don't have the depth to be of value to the individual when his or her needs become greater.

Everyone wants to play on a team of all stars, or be represented by a team of all stars - The best of the best! The Matrix Financial Network is a team of people you can join to benefit others and others to benefit you. People are transformed when they give something of value to someone else. People are transformed when they teach their skills, give welcome advice, friendship, and financial support. The members of the Matrix Financial Network are mentors and deal makers. Good mentors guide someone through the next step to fulfill their purpose. If you have a great idea and have difficulty finding financing, management, marketing then the Matrix Financial Network is for you. Look into our Matrix Strategic Mastermind groups. On line we can be found at www.MatrixFinancialNetwork.com.

Now try the following exercises to experience and define your Matrix Strategic Plan.

"Do the difficult things while they are easy and do the great things while they are small. A journey of a thousand miles must begin with a single step." Lao Tzu

MATRIX STRATEGIC PLANNING

Through the Matrix charts you will be able to organize your Purpose, Brand, Leadership, Clients, MASTER MIND GROUP, financing, and marketing. You will be able to focus on your competition, motivation, legal plan and any other area you choose. Fill out the Matrix charts in this book and also create some of your own. On a scale of 10 to 0 evaluate each employee's ability to complete your company's task. 10 is the best and furthers your companies purpose, 0 is the worst and is a big obstacle for your accomplishing your companies purpose. Then ask yourself what I have to do to have a 10 experience. Only pick the things in which you have control. Evaluate your ability to further your company's purpose. What is the best use of your time? What are you good at? What can you delegate? Then ask what it would take to raise the experience 2 points. You will be amazed at the results from this simple exercise. You can control your state of mind and set up success for yourself and others. The key to success is your state of mind.

"The greatest virtues are those which are most useful to other persons." Aristotle

YOUR PURPOSE AND YOUR BUSINESS PURPOSE

Success begins with you. First you need to define your purpose in life to know where you are going. Why are you in business? Then, you will be able to define the purpose of your organization, your division, or your place in an organization. Business is innovation and marketing.

One purpose of an organization is synergy. Synergy is where two or more people can achieve an effect greater than through individual effort. You need a system to organize the energies of those in your organization. Entrepreneurs need to innovate and have creative entrepreneurs in the organization. Always look for new opportunities and for changes. Then formulate a plan of action to implement the innovation. What can you do better and different than anyone else? Allow anyone in your organization to communicate new ideas. Plan regular meetings to keep communication lines open with everyone in your company. Be innovative in how you do this.

Review the overall purpose of the organization and the specific goals of each project. Is it time for change?

First improve your core business before expanding into new areas. Keep your developmental projects separate from your established ones. These projects will not immediately produce and would bring the performance of other projects down if grouped as one project.

Change doesn't mean change businesses. If you go into an area with which you are unfamiliar you must anticipate a significant time to learn the ropes.

If you buy other businesses, then be prepared to lead them. Existing managers will not necessarily share your vision and may feel insecure.

If you are opening a "start-up" business, you need to know if your product or service will sell. Also look for opportunities. Look for markets that you were not aware of when you started. How will you benefit your target client? Do test marketing to find out which campaign is the best for your product or service. You need to project sales and cash flow. You need to know when you need cash. Too many start-ups would have been successful if they had cash when they needed it. Look one to three years into the future for your cash needs. If your business is in crisis look ahead 1 day, then 3 days, then a week, then a month, then 3 months, then 6 months, then a year. In the beginning cash flow is more important than profits. If you run out of cash your business stops and you never get to the profits. Develop relationships with prospective investors and bankers for your cash needs before you need them. Let them know what you are doing. If you build rapport now it will pay off in the long run when you need it.

Use your master mind for advice. Hire the experts as soon as you can.

What is your company's purpose?

In the 1990's American business was restructured. Xerox, Motorola, Chrysler, General Electric, AT&T, IBM and other Fortune 500 companies dismantled the old hierarchy. They restructured with small entrepreneur units, empowered workers and customer satisfaction processes. The entrepreneur is essential to big business. Large corporations found that they cannot compete without entrepreneurs leading their companies. Companies are eliminating layers of management. They are authorizing workers to make decisions and making sure their work has value. Companies are identifying and responding to customers, and using independent contractors for work that can be done more efficiently outside of the company.

Workers have more input into product change. Engineers are training in marketing and finance. Suppliers help design products. Training and trust are key elements in their success. Everyone is learning new skills to work in this cooperative workplace. These new skills are necessary for success.

A new business model emerged composed of focused work groups with a purpose, which are able to change direction when necessary.

BRANDING

You need to personally brand yourself and also brand your business. When you brand yourself you are independent of your business and others can see your accomplishments. When you brand your business it is independent and can be sold with the business. You need to brand you and your business in social media. People can find information about you and your business which will develop trust. Create your own website and logo. Also create your business's website and identity. Include testimonials.

Put you in the first circle. List all the elements of your brand identity in the next circle. List the social media where you display your personal brand.

Your companies name is a symbol for your company's purpose. Elements of a name need to include what you will do for your client, the concept of your product and a connection with the client. For instance, "Apple" computers implied a small friendly system which distinguished them from the large expensive complicated computers of the time.

Put your unique selling proposition in the first circle. List the benefits to your clients in the next circle. List the ways you promote your companies brand in the next circle.

If you want to be the leader in your field, you need to have name recognition. If you are first to have name recognition you have an enormous edge on your competition. Consistently brand your company

What if you're not the first and there are several companies ahead of you. Flank them. Establish a beachhead that is unprotected or haphazardly protected, unprotected in markets, products or services. Take over that niche market and grow to bigger markets. If you grow to be on top, then stay on top by competing with yourself. Develop your brand.

LEADERSHIP

Not everyone is an entrepreneur or wants to be an entrepreneur. An entrepreneur views a change as normal and healthy, they are always looking for opportunity. Actually, managers most likely have the opposite view. When the operation is functioning well, they don't welcome change. Status quo is important. Increase profit margins and sales are important. Keep on keeping on. The best managers are looking for excellence and want the best. They will improve what they already have. The thought of something not working often translates to the loss of their job, no wonder they don't want to make waves. Good managers preserve the gains you have made and help your company grow. But it is the entrepreneur who will chart your company's course. In fact, the entrepreneur looks for change. Your company needs to recognize change and then determine whether there is an opportunity for your company in the new circumstances.

Management for an entrepreneur is replaced by leadership. Develop leaders in your company who lead by example. The synergy of leaders is much more effective than so called management. The traditional role of management was to report and interpret information to the owners of the company. Now information generation and evaluation is enhanced by computers. Computers instantaneously give the owners and leaders of the company the information they need to make decisions. The key for leaders and owners is to hire people who know more than they do.

The role of leaders is to inspire everyone in the company to further the companies' mission. For example: Total quality management is where everyone in your company concentrates on giving your clients the best quality product or service available. Total quality management is one mission everyone in your company can have and if that isn't their mission have them move on. All information is organized around making the service or product better. Everyone should rate their own work and work product from 10 to 0 wherein 10 being completely satisfied and on purpose and 0 being unsatisfied and hating every minute of work. Leadership meetings need to be focused around everyone's evaluation of themselves, and how they can improve 2 points and eventually experience 10-days every day.

LEADERS

Place your business or department in the first circle. In the second circle write up to seven ways you motivate your company or seven motivators in your company. In the third circle write up to l4 seminars, courses or books you will bring to your company. In the fourth circle, write why you do not motivate your company or its people? Evaluate each element of this chart from 10 to 0 on a monthly basis.

Leaders know where they want to go. They know how to get there and they never give up. Place your business or department in the first circle. Write up to seven key leaders in your business in the second circle. In the third circle write up to l4 up and coming leaders in your organization. In the fourth circle write, why you do not have leaders? Evaluate each element of this chart from 10 to 0 on a monthly basis.

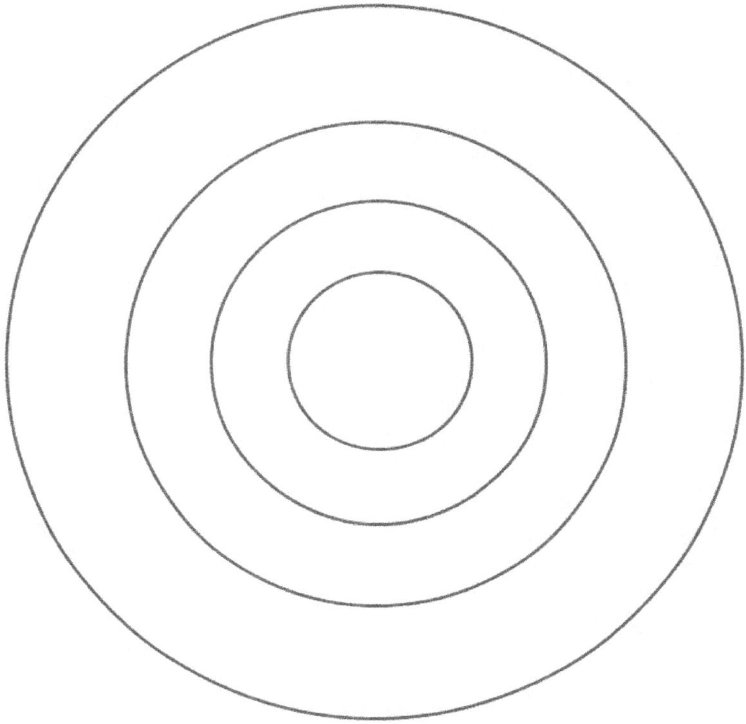

CLIENTS FOR LIFE

A customer is someone who buys once from you. A client is someone who you maintain an on-going relationship. Think of your customers as clients for life. How can you continue to benefit your clients? What your clients want? How can you be the trusted advisor or counselor for life? How can you attract new clients? How can you offer your existing clients, a larger dollar amount? How can you offer higher and better benefits to your clients?

RELATIONSHIP BUILDING

Relationship marketing will make a difference in your business. Your clients are your life blood and you need relationships with them. You are their trusted advisor and are offering them those goods and services that will improve their life. Develop the relationships. Stay in contact with them. Find new products and services to sell to them. Encourage them to stay in touch with your company. As in any relationship give first then be open to receive. Give your existing clients and new clients something for free. This could be information or a guarantee or something that benefits them. Don't expect anything in return. Create a relationship. Give them the best advice and the best product or service. Develop lifelong clients and friends. After you have a relationship, ask for referrals and keep finding products and services that will benefit them. Fall in love with your clients not your product or service.

AVATAR

Focus on your clients. Describe your perfect client. Give him/her a name and an identity: color of hair, face, build, age, sex. List all of their attributes, buying habits, benefits that they are looking for. Who does your client trust? How much can they afford? This is your market. Write your ads and internet copy to attract this client.

MARKET RESEARCH

When you define your Avatar or ideal client you need to know many things. How much do they make, what do they spend their income on, married, single, gender, age, race, what are their buying habits? How big is your overall market? How big is your target market? What percentage of the market is dominated by a competitor? You can get data on your clients by doing surveys. See SurveyMonkey.com and Zoomerang.com to ask potential clients questions. Also, factfinder2.census.gov and fedstats.gov have information about groups.

Do research on your competitors? There are a number of sources to find data on your competitors. See sec.gov, census.gov, hoovers.com, cenus.gov/eos/www/naics/, bls.gov, bea.gov, and trade associations.

Part of deciding what your avatar looks like is to know what groups you want to market to. Will you decide on internet sales, direct sales, business to business, or business to consumer?

You will want to market on social media. Open an account in linkedin.com, facebook.com and twitter.com. Link your social media profiles to your business website. Post something interesting and useful don't try to sell your business or service all the time. People will see through that approach.

NICHE MARKET

Find a small niche market and own that market. Be the expert and the go to person in that market. Look for a market that is unprotected, where there is less competition. After you dominate that market you can expand. Offer a unique selling proposition. Offer something useful that no one else has to offer.

To be a successful entrepreneur you must know trends. Why? Trends are clients. You need clients, and trends tell you what clients want. Many people used to worry about industry telling consumers what they want, that somehow industry was brainwashing consumers into buying the latest fad. Now it is the other way around. Consumers are aware of what they want: Personal service, and convenience. Every business that will survive the next 10 to 20 years must be an art for dispelling certain human miseries. That is the reason why you must watch trends because customers tell you what they want. You need to structure your business so that you will serve others. Conveniences are needed. Healthy foods are needed. Safe water is needed. Luxuries must have a conscience or society will not bestow status on the owner. Furs have gone out of style.

Dream those dreams that help others, that make them less miserable. Then your self-worth flows into your work. Your touching humanity with your work and your role is important to the peaceful balance of our society. Play your part well. Add value where value is needed and you will be successful.

Trends in real estate are essential. Say you are building homes. You need to know the population shifts, where the jobs and roads will be, how much people earn to afford the homes you build. As an investor you need to know about schools, jobs, crime in the area to ensure a stable rental market for your properties.

Determine the trend in your business and then market to the demand.

Your company can start a new trend by identifying a need or want. Then question how other companies are satisfying the need or want. Search for new ways to satisfy the need or want. Market the new solution. You have created a new trend.

Apply the 80/20 principle to marketing. 80% of your sales will come from 20% of your customers. Concentrate on customers you have sold to in the past, they will buy again. Start a quarterly emailing or mailing to your past customers for referrals.

Go to Google.com and look at your competition and what they are saying in their ad copy. Look at their reviews. Usually the best and the worst reviews are most important because they show someone's passion either for or against the competitor. If it's a book go to Amazon.com and look at the titles similar to what you are writing and also the reviews.

You don't have to create a new product or service. Improve an existing one and then create a niche market for it.

What are you selling? Consumers buy usefulness. Determine what is useful to the consumer. Often an image is useful. In what ways will your product be useful to the consumer? Remember people do not buy our products and services they buy how they imagine using them will make them feel.

If you are looking for a new income stream, go to Google down 10 pages or so and look for products or books that are struggling. Contact them and license their product. Then go to successful companies in the field and see if they want the distribution or will joint venture with their email list. Thank Jay Abraham for this idea.

Research the trends in your business. Then design a plan to market to the trend. Supply the demand. If there is a change in demand, then make changes in your supply. Change is the only constant in our society.

LIFETIME VALUE OF A CLIENT

Figure the lifetime value of a client. Figure how much a client buys from you each time. How often and how long? If you make a $100 sale 5 times a year and the client is with you for 25 years, then you have a lifetime value of $12,500. Also, you need to attract new clients and make a sale and then offer to upgrade or sell another useful product or service. Also, you need to increase the frequency of the sales to each client. Give them something to be attracted to you and then be a trusted advisor to find products and services helpful to them.

Reverse engineer where you want to go. If you want $100,000 sales increase you must figure how much each client buys, how often, how long. If you have 1,000 clients, each client needs to buy $100 to get $100,000 sales increase. If you have 100 clients, each client needs to buy $1,000 to get a $100,000 sales increase. Calculate the number of clients and sales to break even and to make a profit. Calculate the cost of client acquisition. It is your marketing budget divided by the number of clients the marketing attracted.

FOLLOW UP

Your goal is to attract clients or traffic to your web site. You want to capture leads by giving something to the client. It could be a coupon, valuable information or something beneficial to the client. Once you have the clients contact information you need to nurture the client. Keep emailing them new information and promotions. You want to make a sale. And once they buy from you make sure you deliver and they are satisfied customers. Then the goal is to have something more to sell to your client. This is an upsell. Then ask them to refer you to their friends and associates. So often companies do not follow up with their clients and sales begin to drop.

MARKETING

Figure how much you want to make this year and put that in the first circle

Then figure how much each sale is worth or how much each client buys in the next circle

Then divide the amount you want to make by the number of client sales and put the number in the next circle

Then figure to sell each client twice as much as before and divide into the goal

Then figure to sell each client three times as much as before and divide into the goal

Place your business or department in the first circle. In the second circle write seven marketing professionals in or out of your organization. In the third circle write up to 14 trends in your business and how you keep up on the trends. In the fourth circle write how your products satisfy the trends. In the fifth circle write up to 14 marketing strategies or concepts your company relies on. In the sixth circle write, why you are not concerned with marketing? Evaluate each element of this chart from 10 to 0 on a monthly basis.

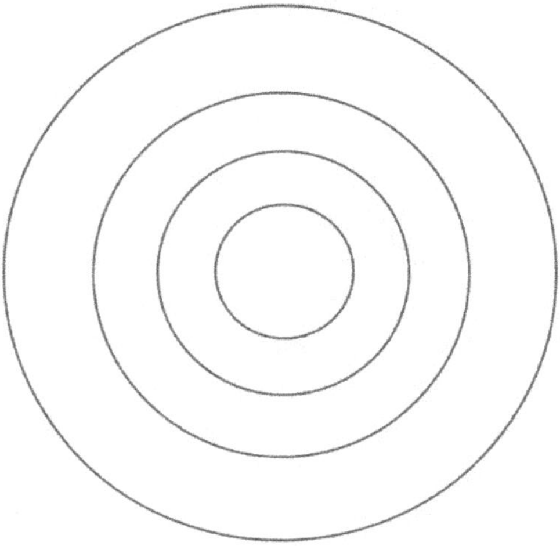

COMPETITION

Place your business or department in the first circle. In the second circle write up to seven people whom you personally compete with. In the third circle write up to 14 competitors of your business, which are the leaders in your industry, and along with their strong points, write their weakness as well. In the fourth circle write how your unique edge is countering the competition? In the fifth circle write how you think the competition will try to beat you and how you will respond. Can you joint venture with your competition? Respect your competition. Let competition push you to new heights. In the sixth circle write, why you do not compete? Evaluate each element of this chart from 10 to 0 on a monthly basis.

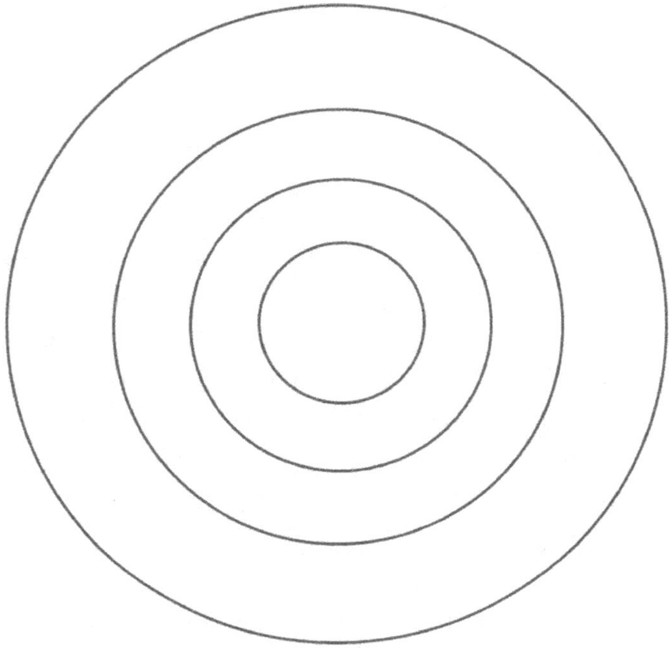

PARTNERS

In the first circle put your name. In the next circle put up to 7 partners you have or have had in your business. In the next circle put up to 14 partners you wish to attract. In the next circle list 7 marketing strategies you are using to attract new partners.

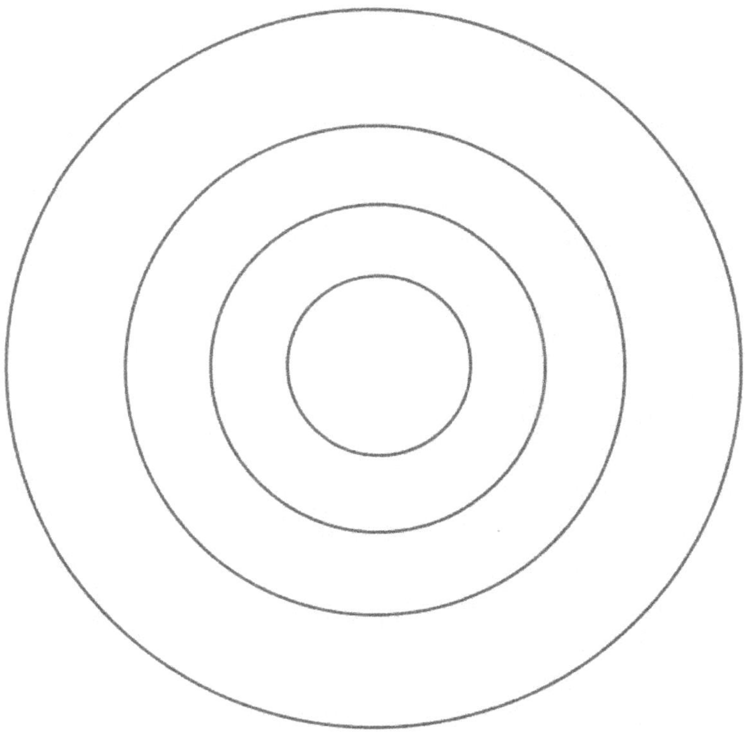

RAISING MONEY

Place your business or department in the first circle. Write up to seven key financial people in your company, investors, crowd-funders, accredited investors, bankers, CPA's, accountants, and brokers in the second circle. In the third circle write up to 14 contacts you have in the financial community. In the fourth circle quickly summarize your short term and long term financial needs. In the fifth circle write, why you do no financial planning? Evaluate each element of this chart from 10 to 0 on a monthly basis.

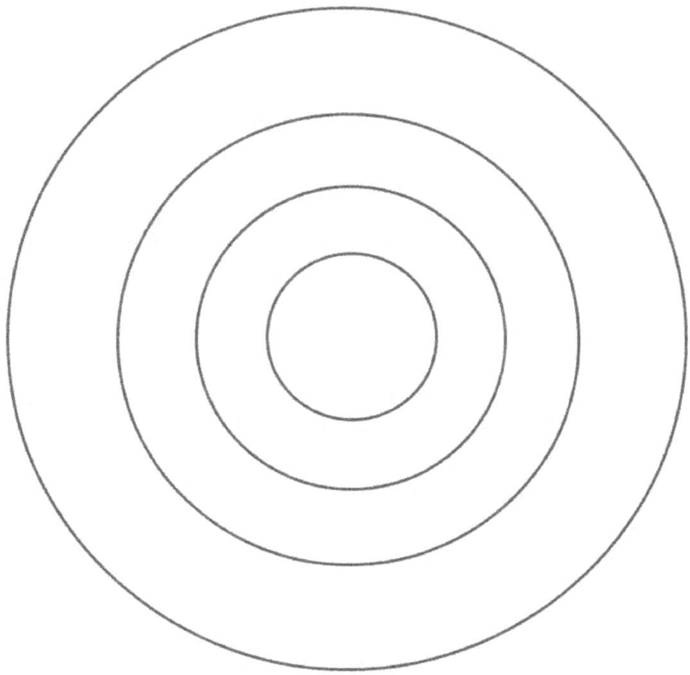

TEAM

Ask yourself and your employees: What have you done to make a difference in your company? What can you do in the future to make a difference in profitability, savings, communication, effectiveness, and personal growth?

Make sure your policies, for salaries and personnel decisions reward the entrepreneurs within your company. You may have other incentives for managers and staff. Look into profit sharing bonuses and cafeteria benefits plans. The cafeteria benefit plans have a lot to offer, everything from health and dental insurance to tax deferred annuities. Your employee chooses how his or her benefits are directed.

Don't have your existing managers and project people try to be entrepreneurs and don't have your entrepreneurs try to be managers of existing projects. People in stable positions do not like to be put in uncertain situations or unfamiliar territory.

KEY PEOPLE

Decide what your most important activities are within your company and match them with key people. Interview many people and check their experience and references.

As you grow, reevaluate your key people. Are they qualified to handle a larger enterprise? How about yourself? Do you have the expertise necessary to do what you do? Objectively evaluate your role. If you find weak spots either learn what you need to know or bring in someone else. Evaluate your role and your employees' roles every month. You need to focus on your best skills and delegate everything else.

Have everyone in your company read this book. It will open your lines of communication and give you tools of success.

Which activities are necessary to further your company's purpose?

Which person in your company fits the activity that is necessary?

Put you in the first circle. Put the next 7 key people and consultants in the next circle. Put the next 14 key people and consultants in the next circle.

Put key activities in the next circle. Put the time for completion in the next circle.

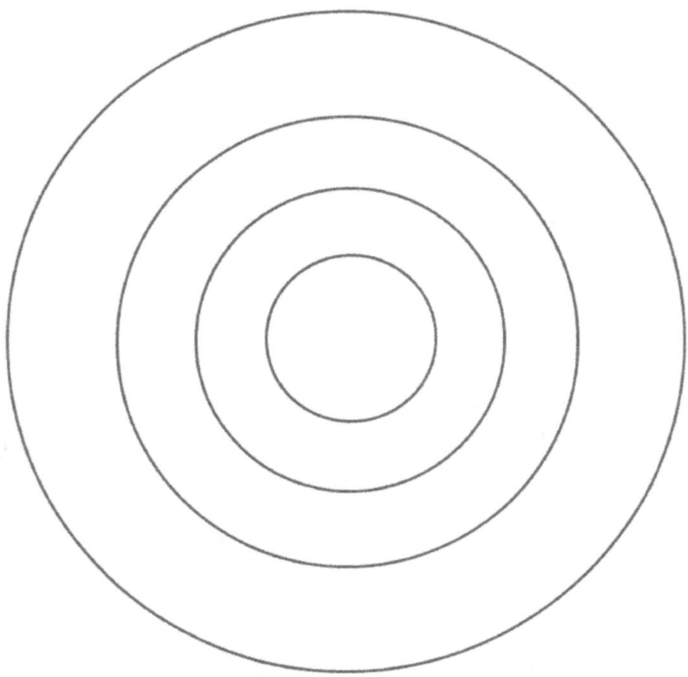

SYSTEMS

In your first circle put your company. In the next circle list your marketing strategies, including client acquisition, client retention, follow up, and up sell. In the next circle list 7 systems you use in your business such as management, communication, accounting, and legal. In the next circle, list details of the systems.

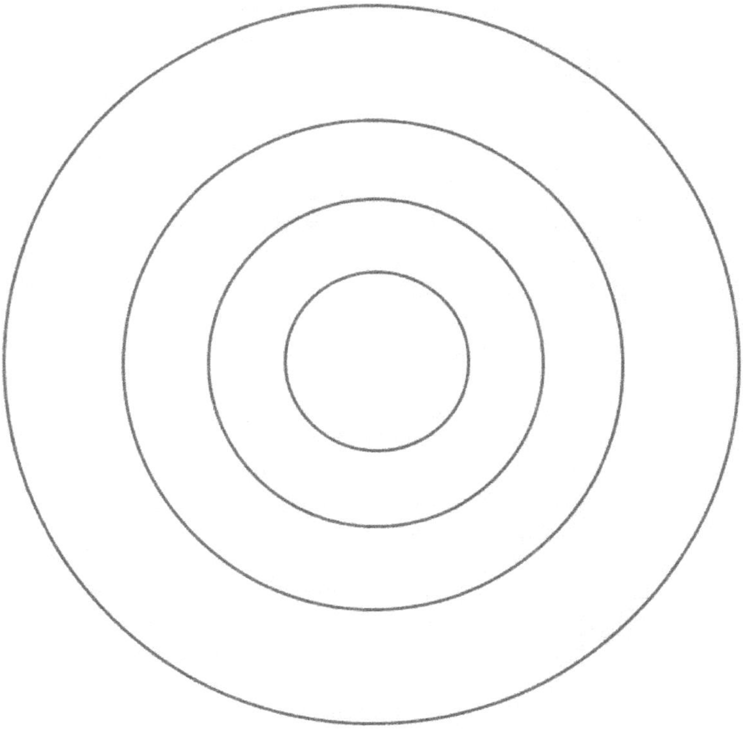

FINANCIAL

You will need to budget your business. Figure out how much you need to startup your business, salaries, fixed operating expenses, project your sales, cash receipts and disbursements.

Figure out your average sale. Are you selling products or services or both? Figure out the average amount each client will buy. Once you estimate your average unit sale, you can then calculate the direct cost per unit and your price per unit. Next figure your gross profit margin. Gross profit margin is the amount of your sales, minus the direct cost of the sales. Check out the industry average. You can estimate the costs of what you're selling and that will help you adjust your price.

You need an income statement, balance sheet, and cash flow statement. The income statement shows how much profit or loss is generated. The Balance sheet shows assets minus liabilities equals owner's equity. The cash flow statement shows the money coming in and out of your business and whether you have enough operating capital.

Also, you or your accountant will need to figure the cost of client acquisition. The cost of client acquisition is your marketing budget or actual expense divided by the number of clients acquired.

Breakeven Analysis. The breakeven point is where your gross margin (sales less the cost of sales) equals your fixed operating expenses. Breakeven: Sales x Gross Margin percentage = Total Operating Expenses. Or if you want to know how many sales you need to break even use this formula: Sales = Total Operating Expenses divided by Gross Margin Percentage.

Financial Ratios. There are a number of financial ratios that are indicators of how well your business is performing. Also, other similar businesses are compared by their ratios. See the following sites for sources of these ratios: BizStats.com, dnb.com, rmahq.org.

Also, track inventory turnover, how long accounts payable are outstanding, and the average days' accounts receivable are outstanding.

You may want to hire an accountant to do the calculations and give business advice based on your statements.

Set up your accounting system. Set up your internal controls, payables, receivables, cost of goods sold, overhead costs, shipping costs. Be sure you have a CPA to implement your system or to review it. Ask for suggestions to refine your system. You can hire people to run the system but bring in the experts to set it up.

Look into accounting software. There are excellent inexpensive systems that make "bookkeeping" fun, and give sophisticated results. Quick Books and others offer excellent systems.

LEGAL

Protect your intellectual property (IP).

Legal Forms. Using legal forms found on the internet may save you money. The best practice is to find a form or contract that you think will do the job and have your attorney approve it. In general, it is less expensive for an attorney to review a form you have found, than to draft a form or contract from scratch. You can Google "Legal forms online" for a number of sites that have legal forms. The following sites are helpful: LegalZoom.com, Nolo.com, RealDealDocs.com, Consusgroup.com, Bizfilings.com, Findlegalforms.com and RocketLawyer.com.

Entities. In any business, it's always a good idea to limit your personal liability by incorporating or setting up an LLC. There are unlimited potential problems that can arise, and you never know who might sue you or why. Sole proprietorships and general partnerships give you no limited liability protection.

One way to protect your intellectual property is to put it in a separate company or LLC. Then license your IP to your operating company. If your operating company gets sued they won't be able to get to your IP.

Non-disclosure Agreements (NDA). These agreements keep your IP confidential. You do not want to disclose to another consultant or joint venture partner or other company your secrets without protecting yourself from them taking your ideas. A NDA will give you recourse to go after them if they violate the confidentiality agreement.

Work for Hire and Invention Assignments. These agreements are for employees and consultants that work for you. The idea is that since you are paying them, anything that they develop is a "work for hire". This means that you have all the rights to the work. Also the assignment is an automatic assignment of all ownership rights to your company for anything that they develop while in your employ.

Employee Contracts and Employee Handbooks. The Employee Contract should state that the company's IP is not to be shared, disseminated or stolen and that it is confidential. The Employee Handbook should repeat what is in the Employee Contract.

Trademarks. Protect your brand by registering a trademark with the USPTO. A brand has many components: company name, logo, tag line, and specific products with unique names. You need to trademark each component. A registered trademark protects you from some other company stealing your identity and stealing your clients.

Copyrights. The good news is that when you write something you have an instant copyright. However, to prove this to the world you need to register your works and content with the US Copyright Office. Also, register the works that your employees or contractors create under your work for hire agreements.

Patents. You can patent your inventions. They must be unique and "non-obvious" and your patent attorney must do a patent search to prove that your product or invention is unique. Utility patents cover anyone who invents a new and useful process, machine, article of manufacture or a composition of matter. A design patent includes an original and ornamental design for a manufactured product. Plant patents go to anyone who produces, discovers and invents a new kind of plant capable of reproduction.

Trade Secrets. Sometimes you may not want to patent something because you would have to disclose a trade secret. The "secret sauce" or Coca-Cola's recipe are trade secrets. You need to keep the secret and protect the secret from your employees through contracts.

Terms of Use. Terms of Use is a legal agreement that your company through its web site enters into with every user of the site. The agreement happens automatically when a user uses your site. It sets forth what the site is for, how it should be used, what constitutes improper use, and what the consequences of improper use will be. Disclaimers of warranties and a limitation of liability and indemnification are usually included in Terms of Use.

Privacy Policy. Any time you are collecting "personally identifiable information" (PII) from your users, you are at risk of violating privacy laws. PII includes names, emails, phone numbers, addresses, birthdays, locations and many other types of information. A Privacy Policy needs to disclose what data is collected and how it is used. There are strict privacy requirements under the Children's Online Privacy Protection Act, or COPPA. This law deals with apps or websites that are likely to attract children under the age of 13 as users, and that collect PII from them.

This book gives general information for informational purposes only and do not provide legal advice. This book is not a substitute for an attorney or law firm. We cannot provide any kind of advice, explanation, opinion, or recommendation about possible legal rights, remedies, defenses, options, selection of forms or strategies. Legal advice is very specific to your circumstances and we recommend that you consult with an attorney for specific advice on any contract matter. Readers should not rely upon information proved as a substitute for personal legal advice. If you have an individual legal problem, you should seek legal advice from a licensed attorney.

Place your business or department in the first circle. Write up to 7 lawyers or legal professionals you know in the second circle. In the third circle write points to cover in your legal preventative plan. In the fourth circle write anticipated legal problems or changes in the law that will affect your business. Evaluate each element of this chart from 10 to 0 on a monthly basis.

CORPORATE LIFE CHART

Try the following exercise. Write down the starting date of your business, then leave space and write down a date 24 years in the future. Write down the highlights and lowlights of your business to date. Ask yourself, which experience did you learned the most from? Often a setback is the stimulus for great success later on. The most successful businesses have learned to "fail their way to success". Now project yourself 24 years from now and look back on your business. What should have happened to you to feel happy about your progress?

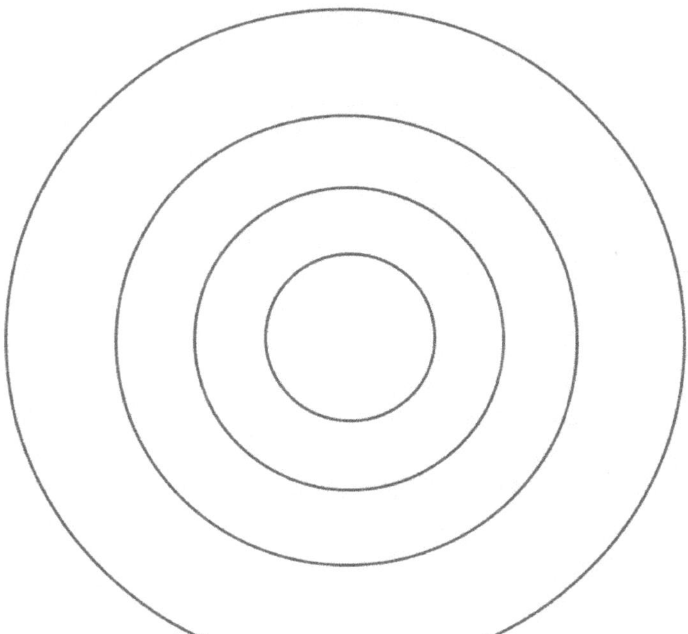

BUSINESS

In the first circle write your business target. In the second circle write up to seven business activities you engage in that will complement your business target. For example, as a real estate investor the following activities complement an investor's target: being a part time real estate agent, broker, mortgage broker, paper broker, developer, contractor, property manager, or appraiser. In the third circle write your contacts in your business universe, contacts which will enhance your business. In the fourth circle write ways you isolate yourself from success. Evaluate each element of this chart from 10 to 0 on a monthly basis.

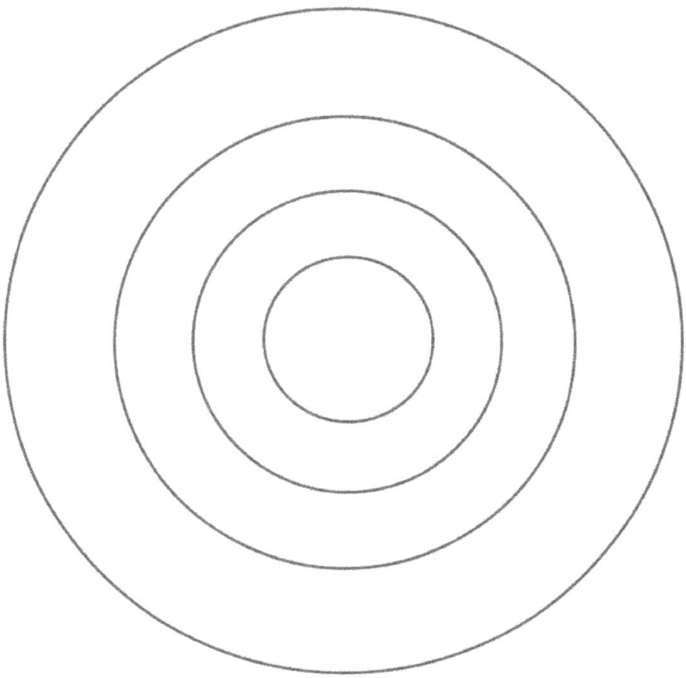

"If your actions inspire others to dream more, learn more, do more and become more, you are a leader." John Quincy Adams

MASTER MIND

Your master mind is your opportunity to tap into all of the knowledge and experience necessary for fulfillment of your commitments in life. There is not time to develop expertise in every area that we need. Most disciplines are so complex that professionals have found they must specialize to be knowledgeable in one area. Specialization applies to you as well. You need to specialize in your commitments, and find the professional expertise to get the job done.

Napoleon Hill points out in his book "Think and Grow Rich" that the wealthy people of his time used the master mind concept. Think of yourself as the coach directing your team of experts to victory.

In business everyone in your company is a part of your Master Mind. Think of your company's purpose and think of everyone in your company concentrating to further your company's purpose. Everyone in your company has a direct impact on your company's purpose.

In real estate you need a team. You are the coach, calling the shots, locating the property, making the deal and managing your wealth. You need knowledge and expertise for the big game. Remember, no matter how many experts you have, you will be calling the shots. Use the experts so you can become an expert in your affairs.

You will want the best experts available to assist you, and you will need the experts before you begin your business. You need experts in your planning phase and as you grow into your implementation phase. The best way is to use consultants. Be prepared for your consultant. Have some detailed questions prepared for your meeting. For attorneys have sample contracts you are interested in reviewing rather than having the attorney prepare your contracts from scratch. However, if the contract you want is extremely detailed it may be less expensive to have your attorney prepare it from the beginning. Nonetheless have the key points written down.

In business you need leaders, lenders, investors, marketing experts, motivation experts, lawyers, and accountants.

In real estate, as your real estate holdings expand you will find that you need a real estate lawyer, an exchanger, a CPA, a property management expert, lenders, good brokers, an estate planner, business lawyer, and partners.

Begin now by using the circle chart and in the first circle write your name. In the next circle write up to 7 people in your MASTER MIND GROUP and in the third circle write the other members of your group. If there are any experts missing write the type of expertise you need.

On a scale of 10 to 0 evaluate what experience you have of your expert's ability to complete your company's task. 10 being the best and furthers your companies purpose, 0 is the worst and is a big obstacle for your accomplishing your companies purpose. Then ask yourself what I have to do to have a 10 experience. Only pick the things in which you have control. Then ask what it would take to raise the experience 2 points.

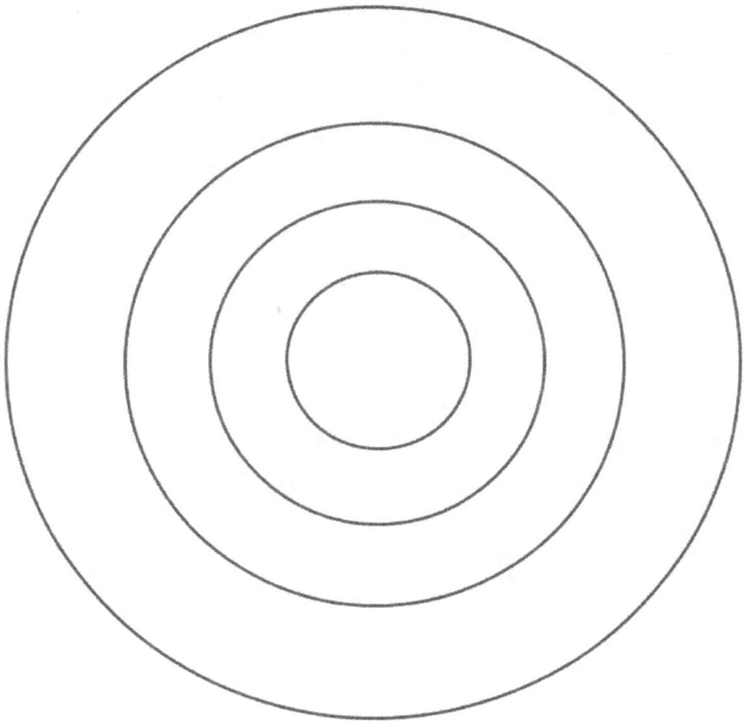

INSPIRATIONAL MASTER MIND

In the first circle write your name. In the second circle write up to seven people, Saints, principles and religions that inspire you. In the third circle write up to l4 people, Saints, principles and religions that are guiding forces in your life. In the fourth circle write what has prevented you from being inspired. Evaluate each element of this chart from 10 to 0 on a monthly basis.

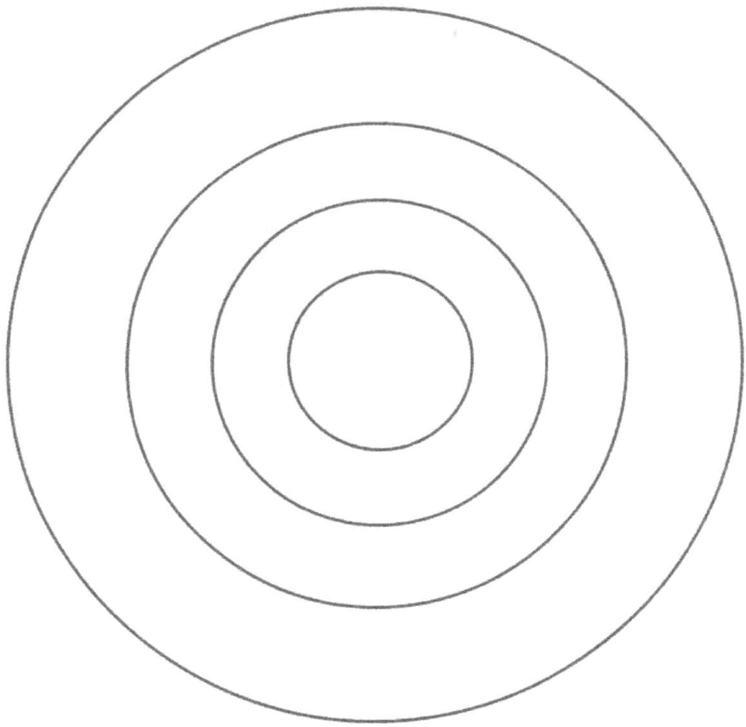

INTELLECTUAL MASTER MIND

In the first circle write your name. In the second circle write up to seven people and concepts you consider as intellectually helpful. In the third circle write up to 14 people and concepts that are secondarily intellectually helpful. In the fourth circle write ways you are not intellectual. Evaluate each element of this chart from 10 to 0 on a monthly basis.

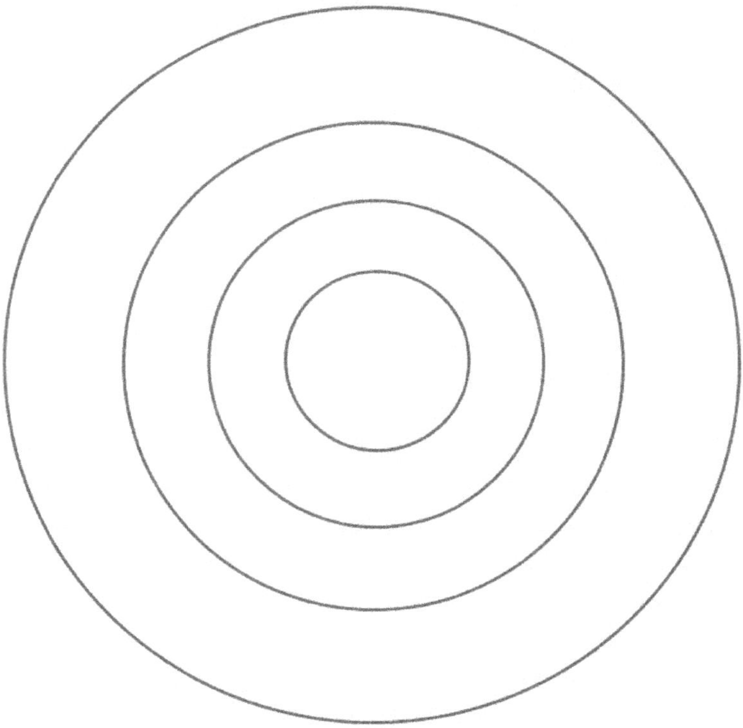

PERSONAL MASTER MIND

In the first circle write your name. In the second circle write up to seven people who assist you in your personal life. In the third circle write up to l4 people who assist you in your personal life. In the fourth circle write, why you don't have assistance in your personal life? Evaluate each element of this chart from 10 to 0 on a monthly basis.

Schedule time where everyone can meet. At the meeting discuss your greatest successes and also your set-backs. Let each person speak. Let everyone contribute to the success of each member. Set goals, and follow up. The mastermind members will hold everyone accountable and also offer solutions to problems.

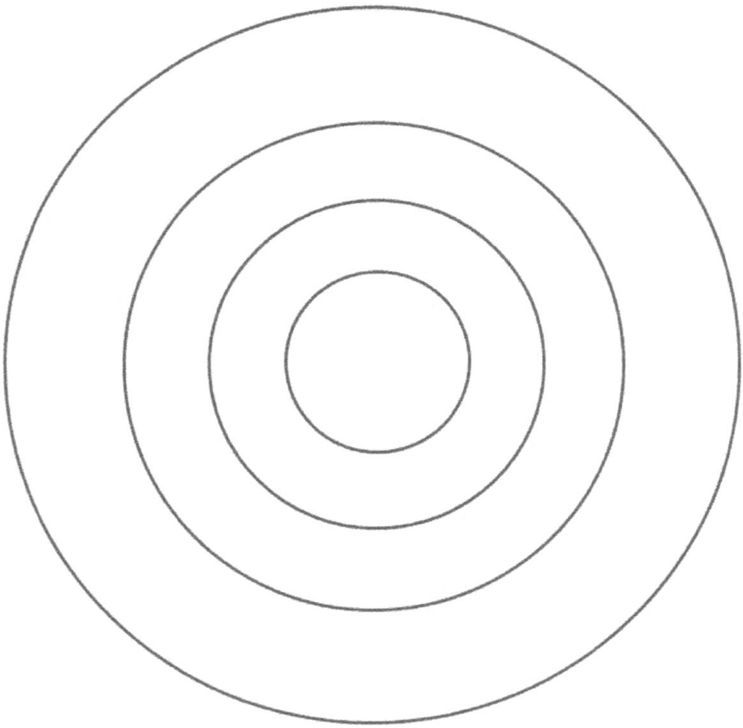

BUSINESS MASTER MIND

In the first circle write your business objective. In the second circle write up to seven professionals who advise you on business. In the third circle write professionals you contact on a regular basis. In the fourth circle write the trade publications you in which you subscribe. In the fifth circle write why you do not develop a MASTER MIND GROUP? Evaluate each element of this chart from 10 to 0 on a monthly basis.

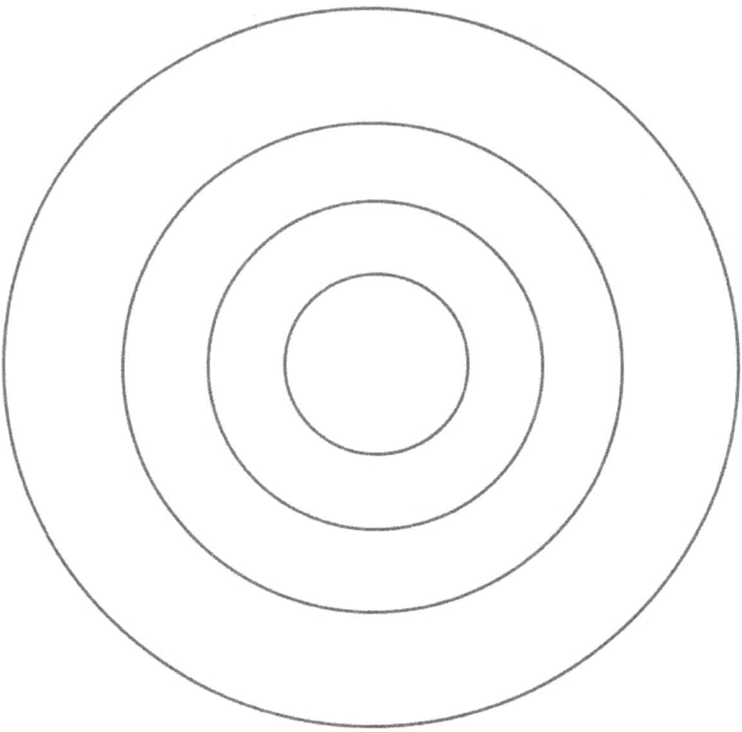

REAL ESTATE MASTER MIND

In the first circle write your Real Estate Commitment. In the second circle write up to seven professionals who advise you on real estate. In the third circle write professionals you want to contact. In the fourth circle write why you do not develop a MASTER MIND GROUP? Evaluate each element of this chart from 10 to 0 on a monthly basis.

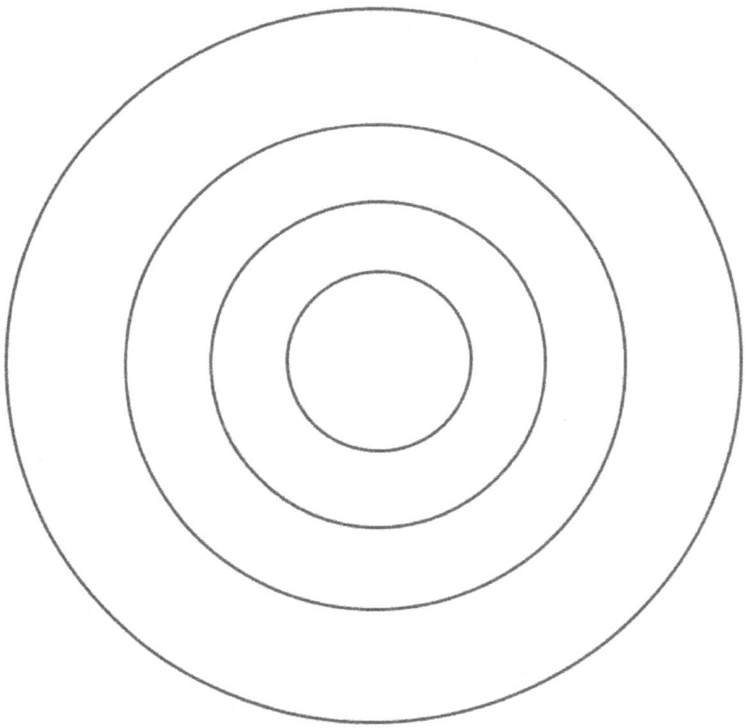

"We cannot solve our problems with the same thinking we used when we created them."
Albert Einstein

FINANCIAL PLANNING

One of the best ways to manage your outward wealth is to manage your inner wealth. Continue to use your MATRIX PLANNER to stay on purpose. Use the Matrix circle charts to chart your outward wealth.

You need to know the cost of client acquisition. Divide you marketing costs by the number of clients you attracted. Did you know that it costs five times as much to attract a new client than to keep an existing one? The first rule of any business is to retain clients and build a loyal relationship with them, and thereby avoid customer acquisition costs.

Let's say you want $1,000,000 in sales this year; you need to figure out how much each client needs to buy to make $1,000,000.

If you have 250 clients, each client needs to buy $4,000

If you have 500 clients, each client needs to buy $2,000

If you have 1,000 clients, each client needs to buy $1,000

If you have 10,000 clients, each client needs to buy $100

Know your cost of goods sold. This is the sum of materials and direct labor to make your product. Divide the costs to produce your product by the number of products you make.

Know your breakeven point. A breakeven point is the revenues need to cover a company's total amount of fixed and variable expenses during a specified period of time.

First complete your 90-day plan. Put your personal cash flow statement together. Record your income and your expenses for the year. Look for areas where you can increase your income and look for areas where you can decrease your expenses. Do you have any debt which can be refinanced to lower your monthly payments?

In business cash flow planning is essential. You need to know in advance what your cash needs are and where you will get them. Start-ups are famous for running out of cash. If you have a good idea in business spend the time backing it up with cash resources. Sales minus (-) expenses equals your profit. If you increase your sales, you should expect an increase in expenses. To increase sales, you must market. Marketing can be expensive, so closely verify results you get from marketing. Test and evaluate each marketing campaign.

All of this activity will be recorded in your income statement and balance sheet. If you have difficulty with accounting, find a professional. Get a CPA. Then hire an accountant on your staff.

Use software programs which analyze your sales, income and expenses. Continue plan one year and three year financial plans. Also update your Entrepreneur Plan which will be detailed in a later chapter.

CREDIT

Credit is an asset. If you don't believe me ask anyone who doesn't have credit! Good credit is used for income producing businesses or real estate. Bad credit is for consumer goods, living expenses and the mortgage on your personal residence unless your home is appreciating faster than your mortgage rate. Get a copy of your credit report and become a credit expert.

You will find that credit is as valuable as cash because if you can borrow in a hurry, you can close that good deal. If your credit has been bad in the past don't worry about it. In business, vendors will extend you credit if you establish good credit with other vendors. Start small and extend your credit lines. Many real estate deals are closed by the owner carrying the paper, meaning the owner accepts your note. Often owners do not care about your credit because if you default or do not pay the loan they get the property back.

Know what your credit report says; order it from your local credit reporting agency. If your credit is good keep it that way. If you get in a pinch know what shows up on your report. Pay your credit cards first and anything that shows up on your report. Utility bills usually do not show up unless they go to judgement.

If you don't have any credit cards apply to department stores first. Buy something small to activate the card, and pay it off. Then apply to Master Card or Visa. Get a cash advance, and use the cash to pay off another card, and build up your credit lines.

BAD CREDIT

If your credit is so-called bad, find out about it. Order your credit report from Experian, Transunion or Equifax on line. First, get a copy of your report. If there are late payments on it act now. Under the Fair Credit Reporting Act, you may have a statement on your file explaining any late payments, moreover, you may request a file updated or clarified. If the file is not updated or clarified within 30 days, the report must be deleted. Either find a credit counselor in the yellow pages or follow the following steps: Write to the credit agency that gave you the report and either record with them a statement explaining the circumstances around your late credit, or better yet, dispute the credit rating. If you dispute it they are required by law to send a request to the credit grantor, department store or whatever, and the credit grantor must respond in 30 days. If they do not respond in the time period, then the bad rating must be dropped from your report. Often the credit grantor is just too busy to respond! So your credit gets improved.

Credit reporting agencies score your credit. They rate open and closed lines of credit and the amount of debt is a factor. After you get a copy of your credit report ask the agency to explain their ratings.

CREDIT

Put the amount of money you wish to borrow in circle one. In circle two place the sources of credit you have. Now in the third circle place the amount of credit from each source. In the fourth circle place the banks or individuals that you will apply to extend your lines. Remember credit lines are just that--don't use credit lines for consumer spending, use them for investing, and when your investment pays off, pay off your credit lines. Then ask for a greater line.

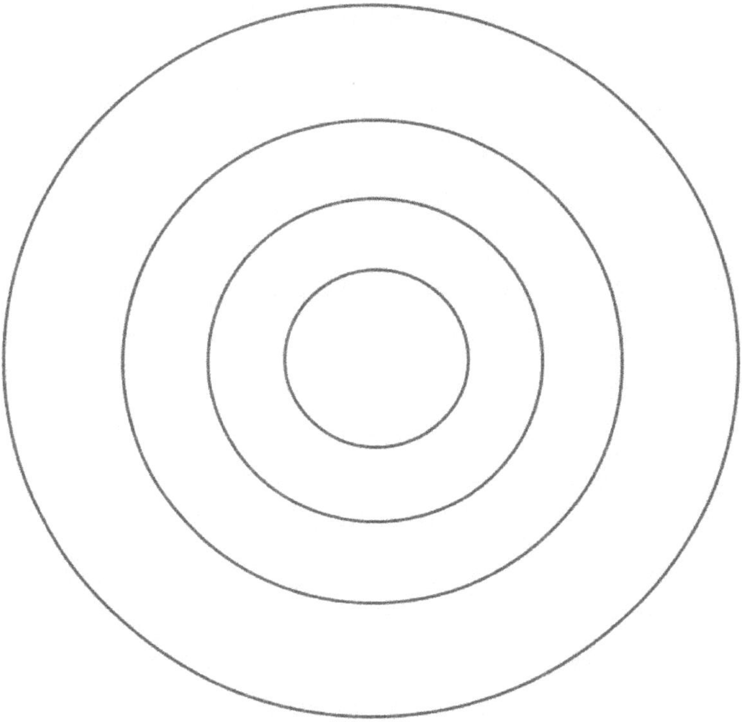

INCOME PROJECTION

It is very important that you project how much you will make this year. Start with a 90-day plan. Then one year. Then 3 years. Have a 24 year-plan to give you an overall view. First, write how much per month you will make from your business, real estate, and add your other earnings. Write your expenses. Subtract your expenses from your earnings for your monthly cash-flow. Next, write how much equity you will accumulate this year and for the next three years. Visualize your next deal. Next, visualize your next 10 deals. OK, now you have your cash flow goal, and your net worth goal, for the next year, and the next three years.

State your commitment. What are you prepared to do?

Write the method or learning process which helps you achieve your goal.

Evaluate your experience. Is there any expertise you do not have? Who is on your MASTER MIND TEAM? Who can you get to fill any holes?

Evaluate the time, and energy you are willing to spend.

Evaluate how much money you will need, and sources of financing.

State additional knowledge you will need, and how you will get it. Write the names of the courses and seminars you will attend, and the books and tapes that you will study.

Write a definite date to fulfill your commitment.

Introspection - Write the result of this process. Make this evaluation every day for the first month. Then evaluate the same once a week and finally make this evaluation once a month.

LONG RANGE

In the first circle write your name. In the second circle write your long-range business goals. In the third circle list the businesses and properties you own and control. In the fourth circle decide which businesses and properties to keep, which ones to sell, which ones to refinance to pull money out, and which ones to trade.

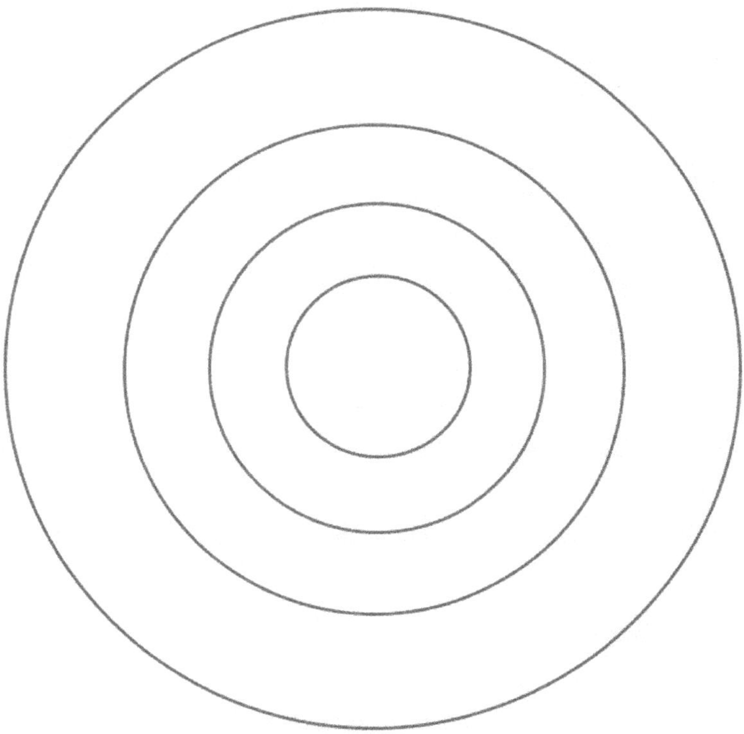

PUT IT ALL TOGETHER

In the first circle, write down your name, and if you have one, your investors name. In the second circle, write your and your investor's immediate business goal. In the third circle write down the business or property you have found. In the fourth circle evaluate the business or property. In the fifth circle, write key deal points to write your offer, or to start your business.

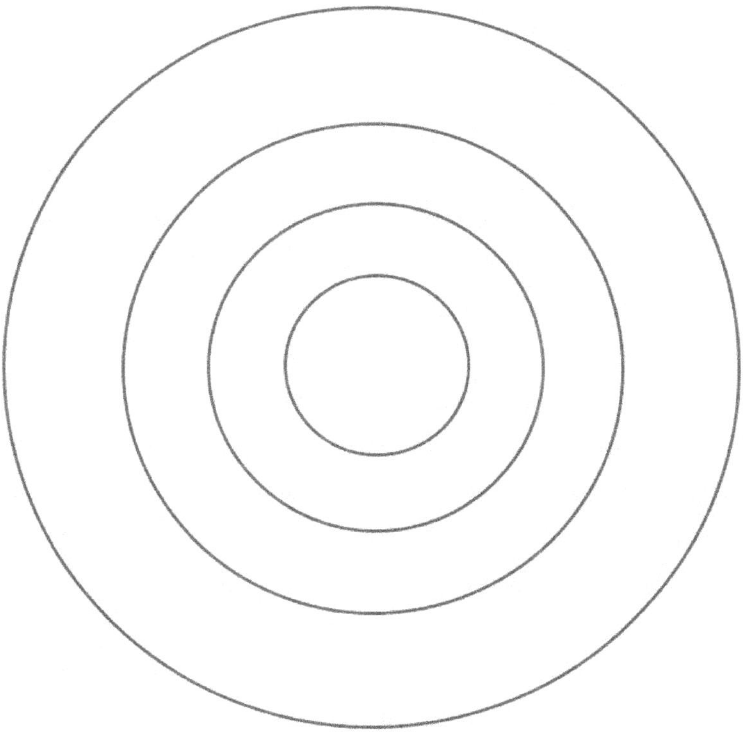

ADD VALUE

Add value where value is needed and you will be successful. When you meet someone add value. Help them out with what they need. Don't ask or expect anything in return. You will find what goes around comes around.

Today you can use your mind to create value; your mind and creativity becomes working capital that will attract investors. When you are starting a business or purchasing a business you will need to attract investors. Start-up money is difficult to get. Use your business plan to get start-up money. A venture capitalist is someone who puts up cash for a piece of the action, often a controlling interest in your company. If you have a hot product or service, you will want control over your business. Offer your investor royalties, which are a percentage of your income, or a percentage of each good or service sold instead of equity in your company. Put a time limit on the deal and see your business lawyer to draft the agreement.

In the first circle list how much money you want to borrow. Next, in the second circle, list up to 7 friends, relatives, or investors from whom you can borrow money. In the third circle list up to 7 terms that you could offer to make the loans attractive, include royalty agreements. In the fourth circle list the personal attributes that you have which will attract people to make the loan. In the fifth circle list your personal attributes which will cause people to become disenchanted with you, and refuse to loan you money. List your greatest fears, including the fear of rejection, and what you need to do to improve. Evaluate each element of this chart from 10 to 0 on a monthly basis.

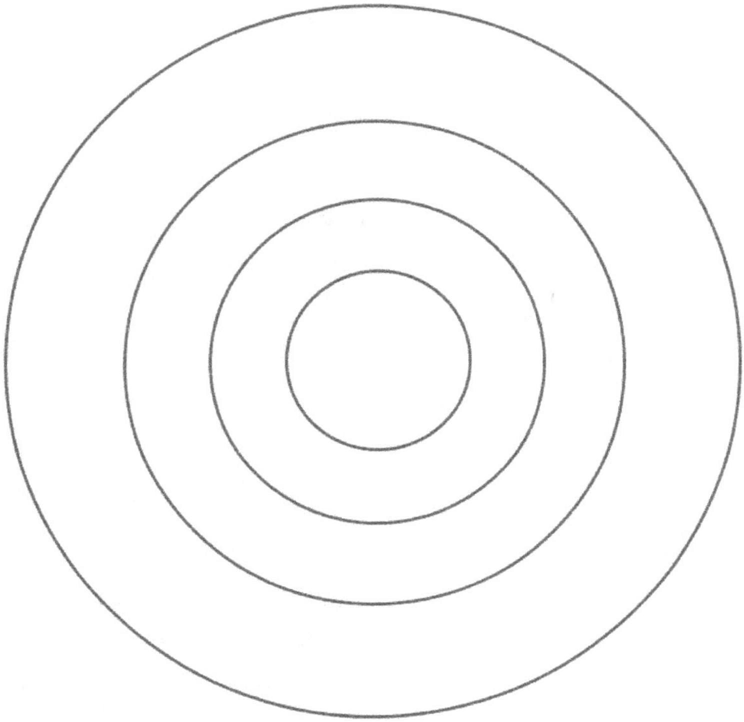

"When you are content to be simply yourself and don't compare or compete, everyone will respect you." Lao Tzu

MATRIX ENTREPRENEUR PLAN

Most people do not follow a business plan. Statistics show that most businesses fail within their first 5 years. Is there a connection? Yes! Many people might develop a business plan to get financing or to get started but then abandon the plan. The Matrix Plan is a plan to get started and a plan to stay on course. The Plan helps you determine the amount of financing you will need and when you need it, it gives you lenders important information about your business. You are in control of the Plan and you are in control of where your business is heading. Your plan becomes your master map of where you want to go, and it tells how you will get there. You will include options to challenges that can arise. The plan becomes a master leadership directive. Your plan is a statement of the purpose of your organization. Communicate this plan to everyone on your team, and align your purposes. You can teach members of your team how fulfill the purpose of the organization through the plan. Have progress meetings and ask team members for refinements to the plan and your business on a regular basis. Your plan will be one of the most important elements in your bankers or investors decision to back you.

Learn to present your plan in the best way for a given audience. You may want to break it into segments for your staff.

You may want to highlight certain elements for investors. The following are the elements in an Entrepreneur Plan:

Cover sheet:

For investors and bankers use a cover sheet. Use your letterhead and include the name of the business, address, telephone numbers, contact persons and their title and an explanation of their relationship to the company. Briefly describe your purpose, business goals, opportunity, and market demand. Note the amount of capital necessary and the amount of funds needed in the future. You may need a statement of confidentiality in certain types of public offerings. If you are offering to sell stock, see your attorney before you make any offers.

Table of Contents:

This is an overview for your reader and it shows to your reader you are organized.

Executive Summary:

This is your first impression of your plan, make it good. This is a summary of your entire plan, so write it after you are completed with your plan. Include the purpose of your business, what advantage you have over your competition, your income projections, your capital needs, and how and when you will repay your investors. This is just a page or two. The goal of the summary is to get the reader to read the rest of the plan.

Business Opportunity:

Write about your industry, its market and trends. Write about new technology, economic trends and future growth of the market.

Write how your business will fit in. What is the need in the market? How can you supply the need? Include your mission statement and your vision for your company. You need to present specific goals and objectives in a time frame.

Company Summary:

State the nature of your business and its purpose. Describe who the company is and what it stands for. Describe a history of the business and where it is located. Describe the leaders in your business, their qualifications, background and also include your master mind group. Write what is unique about your business and why you will succeed in your market. Describe the legal structure, leadership structure, and operational structure. Discuss your test marketing, results and control of any proprietary information. Include your contracts, agreements and presales.

Operation:

If your business is service or retailing describe the following needs: staff, equipment, office and retail space, accounting system, purchasing system, inventory system, training, and capital. If your business is manufacturing describe the following needs: office and manufacturing space, accounting system, staff, equipment, materials, inventory, supplies, suppliers, production costs, and capital.

Products and Services:

Market - Describe in detail your market. Describe what your clients want, their demand, and their future demand. Describe how your products and services benefit your clients. Describe why you are competitive and how your price points fit into the market. Describe your unique selling proposition.

Sales - A business is sales minus expenses. Describe the consumers of your products and services, and the basis of their demand for your products and services. Describe the size and population of your market, the demographics. Describe how you can satisfy your markets demands. Describe how you attract, nurture, sell and retain your clients. Describe how you can maintain your current business while expanding.

Challenges and Strategies:

Describe the challenges you will face. Are there less expensive products on the market? Is your product or service in a trend which is almost over? What effect would a slow economy have on your product? Will financing be more difficult in the future? What license requirements do you have? What effect does government regulation have on you? Are you protected with copyrights, patents and trademarks?

Competition:

Who are your competitors? What are their strengths and weaknesses? Describe the advantage you have over your competitors. Describe the tactics that your competition will try to force you out of the market and how you will respond. Look for ways to joint venture with your competition. Maybe you can use their distribution or client list to market your product. Maybe you can market their product through your distribution or client list.

Marketing Plan:

Use the marketing information you developed in the structural chart earlier in the book. Describe your avatar. Who are your clients, can they and will they buy? Include trends in your business, and how your strategies will take advantage of those trends. Describe any test marketing and market research you have done. Describe your client acquisition strategy and how you will deliver to your clients. Discuss your pricing and what it is based on. Include elements of cost, client acceptance, competitors pricing, and market research. Describe price, promotion, products and place. Describe your timing, marketing budget, guarantee, return policies, packaging, and point of purchase (POP) displays. Discuss the professionals you will utilize to implement your plan and how you will monitor the results of your campaign. Finally describe a backup plan.

Management Team:

Describe the key members of your team. Include summaries of their backgrounds and experience. Full resumes can be attached in the appendix.

Are your nondisclosures binding? Do you have strong enough leaders on your team to get the job done? Are you developing new leaders? Who will replace the leaders you have? When? Describe your personnel policies, on minority issues, disabilities, part-time and full time, benefits.

Financial Plan:

Income Projection - Complete a 1-year income projection based on your marketing plan. Do a best case, worst case and an expected case projection. Then do a 3-year projection. Every 6 months update these projections based on current data. You will keep your plan current and the plan will give you direction for the future. Include some key ratios described in this book.

Cash Flow Projection - Forecast your income less expenses. Only use cash items to project the cash flow leave out depreciation. This gives you the information to run your business on a day to day basis as well as month to month, year to year. Do the projection for one year, best case, worst case, and expected case. One reason of business failure is that their leaders fail to anticipate cash needs and they fail to plan how to obtain the cash.

Balance Sheet:

A balance sheet displays your company's assets less the liabilities equals the owner's equity. As your company grows your equity will increase. Typically, lenders like to see as few liabilities as possible.

Timing:

Timing is everything. Describe when you expect new funding is necessary. Describe how your marketing plan will unfold. Note your production dates and delivery schedules. This plan will show the reader how you can focus all of the elements of your business into a venture which will sustain on its own and make a profit. Include cost of goods, cost of client acquisition, and break even analysis.

Resources:

State how much funding you need and when. Describe how the funding will be utilized, how and when it will generate a profit and how and when it will be returned to the investor.

Exit Plan:

IPO? Sales? Profit? Management? Buyout? What will the investors make?

Appendix:

Use an appendix for copies of contracts, references, biographies, bibliographies, charts, supporting documents and footnotes.

Matrix Plan Outline

Cover Sheet

Table of Contents

Executive Summary

- Purpose
- Benefits to your clients
- Unique selling proposition

Business Opportunity

Company Summary

- Operation
- History
- Ownership

Products and Services

- Description
- Literature

- Next line and upsell
- Challenges, Strategies
  - Value Proposition
  - Unique selling proposition
  - Pricing
  - Promotion
  - Distribution
  - Sales
  - Alliances
- Competition
- Marketing Plan
  - Avatar, ideal client
  - Market needs, trends, growth
  - Industry trends, growth
- Management Team
  - Organizational structure
  - Team
  - Outsource
- Financial Plan
  - Income Projection
  - Cash Flow Projection
  - Balance Sheet
  - Break even
  - Client acquisition

Timing

Resources

Exit Plan

Appendix

There are many resources for business plans. See *Bplans.com*, *Liveplan.com* and *Businessplanpro.com*

Use your business plan as a tool. Update it on a regular basis. Evaluate your progress. On a scale of 0 to 10 grade how you expect each element of your plan will unfold. Then ask yourself what it would take to raise the grade 2 points to 5 points. Then ask yourself what it would take to have 10 grades in each category. Only pick the elements you have control over. As you evaluate your plan you will expose any weaknesses you can see in it. Then you have an opportunity to strengthen it before you give it to an investor.

Technology:

Use the latest software to do your projections, and calculate your balance sheet ratios. Then you can update easily and ask what if questions.

Presentation:

You want your plan to look conservative, and well-prepared. Use a quality binder. Don't make it look lavish; your investor will think you are a big spender.

The next step is to incorporate your business plan into a private placement memorandum (PPM). There are several exemptions under the securities laws which allow you to solicit accredited investors as long as you qualify them, Reg. D 506C. It's best to hire an attorney to advise you on the securities laws and how to structure your offering.

BUSINESS PLAN

In the first circle write business plan. In the second circle write the keys of your executive summary. In the third circle write the keys to your management section. In the fourth circle summarize your financial projections. A VC will not read past these 3 items unless they are good. Keep your plan 10-15 pages, and remember you will only get one shot at your presentation.

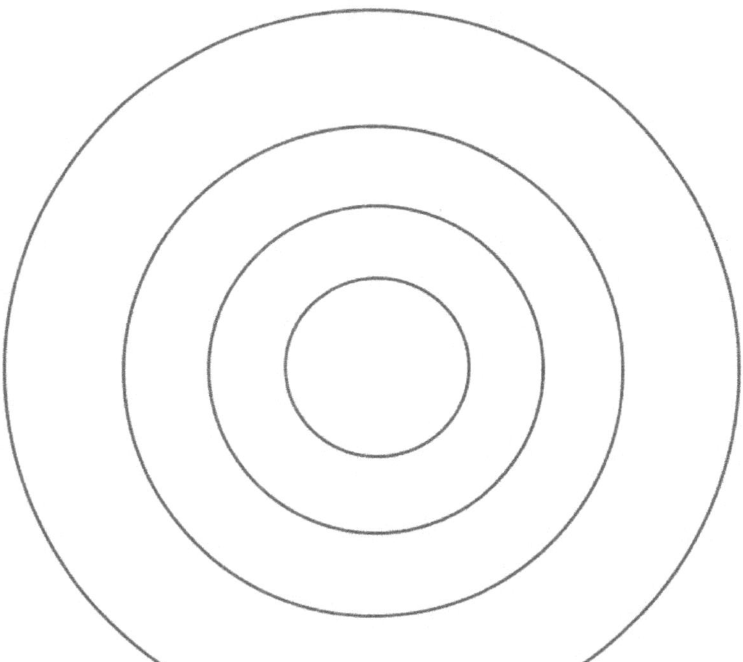

STOCK

In the first circle write stock. In the second circle write the founders of the company stock split. In the third circle write the option pool split for key employees. In the fourth circle write details of your shareholder agreement. Check to see that you have the right to repurchase share from those who leave the company.

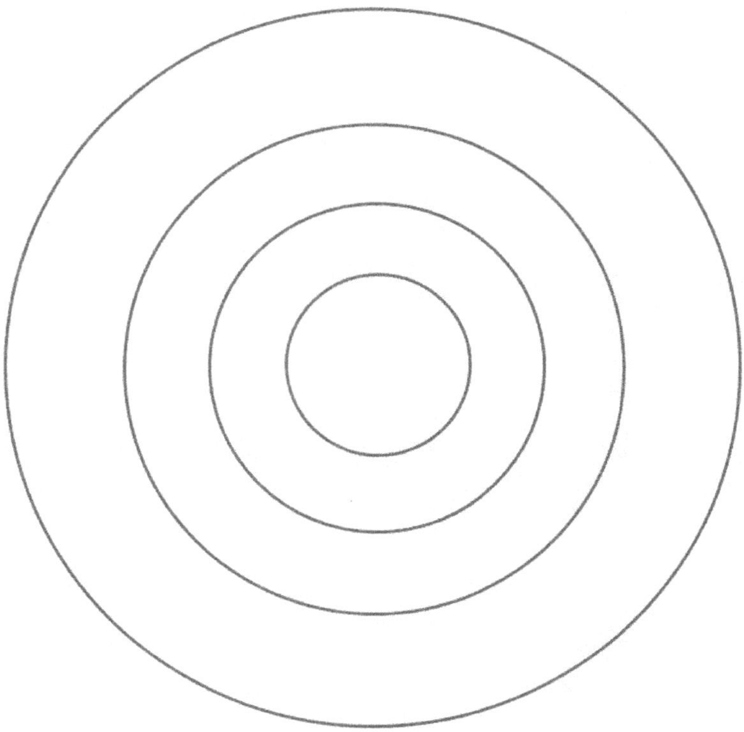

CAPITAL

In the first circle write capital. In the second circle write your best source of capital: angels, loans, limited stock exemption, VC's, go public, IPO, joint venture, technical partner, buyout, strategic alliance, share technology, Matrix Financial Network. In the third circle write your plan to get the capital you need.

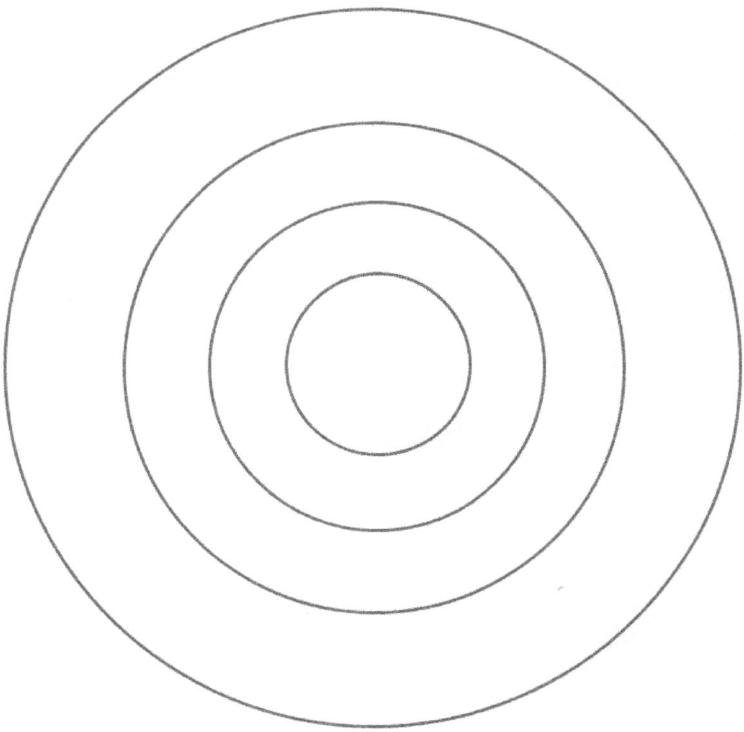

"Respond intelligently even to unintelligent treatment" Lao Tzu

NEGOTIATION

Think of negotiation as storytelling. Your job is to create a story where all the characters believe that they get what they want, there is a common theme and a chain of events where the story becomes reality. Your story needs to fill the gaps better than the other sides' story. Be committed to your story and its outcome. You need to generalize the facts of the story and tie them together so everyone benefits.

There are basically two types of negotiators, cooperative deal makers and uncooperative bullies. Most people are deal makers. Some are bullies. You need to know how to deal with both types to put deals together. Two deal makers generally work toward putting the deal together, they listen to each other and they look forward for win-win solutions. Deal makers can negotiate with a bully. The bully is looking for a win lose deal. He or she wants to win and wants the other side to lose. Bullies are aggressive, they do anything to win, they stretch the truth, they lie, they make demands, they make unrealistic demands, and they ask for the moon if you don't shut them up, they yell, they enjoy bullying an "opponent" more than they enjoy putting a deal together. You probably know some of these negotiators.

HOLD YOUR GROUND WITH A BULLY

Mirror them. If they ask for something you ask for something. Keep it reasonable. If they use ugly aggressive tactics refuse to negotiate any further until they discuss the merits of the situation, however keep communication open with them. Talk to them about other matters. Widen the playing field; it takes the heat off the current issues. Often you must educate them on the issues being negotiated because they don't know.

The key to NEGOTIATION is to know what you want, leave some room in your offer and MAKE YOUR OFFER. If your offer isn't accepted, don't take it personally, try a different approach. Develop your creativity. Any good negotiator will tell you that you need to be both cooperative and aggressive to put deals together. The advantage of you making the first offer is that you set the tone, and range of negotiation. The advantage of letting the other side make the first offer is that you know something about what they want.

BUILD RAPPORT

For deals to work all parties must win. WIN-WIN negotiations work. If you want price and terms you must find conditions the other party wants. You must solve a problem for the other party, and you must find out what the problem is. To find out, you must listen. Listening is one of the keys to negotiation. Once you know what the other party is looking for, then you can use your creativeness to find a way to make it work for both of you. Most people think money is the only issue. It isn't. Ask the person what they want, what their goals are, where they want to go. Think up solutions which meet their needs. Use your resources to satisfy their needs by spending as little of your own money. Listening, and caring about the other person is building rapport. Rapport is also building some trust so the other person can count on you coming through. If you are asking for seller financing and you do not build a relationship during your negotiations, then how can you expect the seller to loan you the money? The seller needs to trust you to loan you money.

MIRROR

How do you build trust and rapport? One way is to mirror your partner. Dress appropriately and act like he or she does. If you are talking with a banker, it is probably best to wear a suit, and act like the banker. Bankers act organized, and logical. Know the elements of a loan package that the banker wants and present it that way. Try playing "monkey see; monkey do" with your banker. If he crosses his legs, you do the same. If she looks relaxed, you do the same. Most of the times the person you are mirroring will never know. It's amazing.

DIVIDE AND CONQUER

When you are negotiating a transaction, divide it into parts and negotiate each part. Be sure you identify the points of the deal that may matter to the seller and do not matter to you. If you give the seller something he or she wants be sure to get something you want. Always ask for things you do not want, they are easier to give up! But do not ask for ridiculous things, because you will lose credibility. Always build your credibility.

Multiple notes are a good way to divide and conquer. Say you are trying to buy a property from an estate and the estate has 4 heirs. If you offer one note the heirs may not trust each other enough to feel comfortable that they will each get paid. So offer 4 separate notes, one to each heir and use one deed of trust to secure all of the notes. You divide up the interests and negotiate with each interest separately.

Always give the other person room to win. Always make your offer lower than your bottom line. When you come up in price or terms the other side appears to win. Know what your bottom line is. If you cannot get your bottom line, WALK. Always be able to walk away from any negotiation. Don't ever force yourself into a deal you don't want. The person who cares the least about the deal usually gets the best deal.

HIGHER AUTHORITY

Always have a partner you must consult when you are negotiating. It could be your spouse, a relative, anyone. If you have someone you must consult with it will give you an excuse for more time to think about the deal, or your partner could be a "bad guy". The "bad guy" doesn't like the terms; the repairs that need to be done, or whatever may come up! This allows you to be the "good guy", "helping" to compromise.

LIMITED LIABLILITY

Meet with your business lawyer about setting up your corporation or limited liability company (LLC) for limiting your liability. One of the most important reasons to incorporate is to limit your personal liability. If your company is sued it will insulate your personal assets from being attached. It is essential that you maintain the separate status of your corporation or LLC. Have separate bank accounts, and do not commingle corporate money with your personal money. If you do commingle accounts your corporate status could be broken, or the corporate veil could be pierced. If you lose your corporate status you will have personal liability for the actions of your corporation. Your attorney will give you additional advice about maintaining your corporate status.

In this litigious society be sure you adequately insure all of your business ventures and properties. Get a personal liability umbrella policy for at least one million dollars or more. You'll be surprised that this type of policy can be purchased for a few hundred dollars per year.

Also there are excellent tax advantages by owning your own corporation or an LLC. Look into limited liability companies, limited partnerships, family trusts, and trusts to hold property. You can hold property in a trust and no one will know that you have an interest.

Once you have worked hard to build your portfolio, and have balanced your liquid investments with your growth assets such as real estate, then you will want to insulate your portfolio from as much risk as possible. Be sure all of your real estate is insured properly. Talk with your insurance agent. Always get quotes for additional liability coverage.

ASSET PROTECTION

Asset protection is to build a financial fortress to protect your assets. There are risks in owning businesses. You want to shield your personal assets from any risks from your business.

The building blocks are entities. The entities include limited liability companies (LLC's), corporations, limited partnerships and trusts. LLC's and corporations limit your liability. The idea is that if the company gets sued they can't come after your personal assets. The other idea is not to own anything in your name. Put your assets into limited liability entities.

A trust has value in that it doesn't need to be recorded so no one knows who owns the trust. However, a trust does not have any asset protection. Often you use a LLC to be the beneficiary in the trust to limit your exposure.

If your purpose in life is expressed in your corporation then seeing your corporation continue in your absence will be satisfying. Be sure you have strong leaders to keep your company moving toward its purpose. Remember that along the way contribute to other causes in your life. Give support in any way you can including financial support. Be careful who you entrust and empower with your mission.

Once you have thought about your business plan, the next step is to plan your asset protection. Again, express your mission in life by giving to those individuals and organizations important to you. See an attorney who will help you implement your plan. Be sure you look for an attorney who specializes in asset protection.

Identify your mission in life, and allow your mission in life to guide you in deciding who your estate will impact when you move on. You may be able to create generational wealth. Of course you may come to the same result of passing your wealth to your family but keep in mind one of the success principles, being generous. I encourage you to give a portion of your estate to a charitable organization or a cause you have supported through your mission in life. Allow the love for your family to expand to others in the world. This is the foundation of peace in the world. Remember your inner wealth is freely given, so give freely of your inner wealth.

A living trust is popular because you put your entire estate into a trust, you are able to control it or change your beneficiaries, just like in a will and you will bypass expensive probate. A living trust is tax neutral meaning there are no advantages or disadvantages to it. The laws in this area change every year which makes it important to consult your asset protection attorney. To save estate taxes consider a charitable remainder trust. If you make a gift to charity it is removed from your estate and therefore not taxable. In addition, you may make gifts of $10,000 to individuals to reduce your estate. The qualified personal residential trust allows you to give your residence to a beneficiary at a discounted basis. Say you know you want to give your residence to you children and you estimate you have 5 years to live. The property will be discounted to present value based on the fact it will not be received for 5 years and the discount and the gift will reduce the value of your taxable estate. When your children receive it they can decide to rent it to you, or you may want to make an exempt gift of the rent for the number of years you stay there. Again there are additional rules which are too complicated to discuss here so, consult your attorney if this sounds interesting to you.

An off shore trust may offer you some asset protection because the governments that accept these kinds of trusts have laws that say creditors will have a difficult time attaching the trust property. Again be sure you consult with an expert.

There are several states, including Nevada, that have created Asset Protection Trusts. These trusts operate much like off shore trusts. These trusts can hold your LLC's or Corporations. The principal of these trusts are protected from outside creditors. You will need to consult with an attorney that specializes in formation of these entities.

There are some excellent trusts available to benefit your heirs and your missions. These trusts also minimize your estate taxes. You can either give a significant part of your estate to the IRS or to the people and organizations that are important to you, it's your choice.

"Being deeply loved by someone gives you strength, while loving someone deeply gives you courage." Lao Tzu

WEALTH

Wealth works in three stages: creation of your wealth, preservation of your wealth, and creation of your legacy.

When you are creating your wealth you will be making deals, and building your estate. Creating wealth through business and real estate is just as important as creating personal wealth from within. Be open to your inner wealth. By opening the door to your inner balance and peace, you will find doors opening in the external world around you.

Will material wealth alone suffice? No. Think of people you know who are so called wealthy. Are they happy or Peaceful? Loving? If not, then these so called wealthy people are not really wealthy. Wealth comes from within, not from without! Wealth comes from your inner being, not from the external world.

Financial independence has been promoted as the ultimate goal of business and investing. Financial independence is a false prophet. Your ultimate goal is fulfilling your commitment, your purpose in life. You are unique and you are here for a special purpose, YOUR PURPOSE. No one is more qualified to play your role than you.

The second stage is preservation of the wealth you have accumulated. Here you have heard countless stories of rags to riches and riches to rags. We want to hear you have eliminated the riches to rags part of the story by preservation of your wealth, once you have accumulated it.

Develop your inner wealth consciousness to preserve your inner wealth. Your inner wealth is the most important. Why do outwardly wealthy people sometimes needlessly lose fortunes? They sabotage themselves. They know deep down they are failures and do not deserve the "wealth" and find ways to prove themselves right and they lose their "wealth". If you develop your inner wealth you cannot lose it. You can pretend that it is not there, but deep down you know it is there. You can see it in others even though others around you may be "asleep" and not aware of their inner wealth. Criticism and anger with others is basically criticism of yourself and anger with yourself. You must preserve your inner reservoir of wealth before you can preserve your outer wealth.

You preserve your outer wealth through sound leadership decisions; you limit your liability as much as you can through insurance, LLC's corporations, and trusts. The key to preservation is to stay on course, stay on your purpose. After you have created a positive cash flow do not divert the positive cash flow into an off purpose endeavor which could drain your inner and outer resources. Retain control over your business. In real estate, stay away from blanket loans. A blanket loan is where the lender uses several pieces of your property to secure one loan. If you have difficulty with the loan payments the lender can wipe out all of the properties at once!

We want to hear of your story, rags to riches, and the creation of your legacy. Your legacy is your impact on the world after you move on. Here you will be concerned with asset protection, estate taxes, and possibly charitable trusts for your works to continue. You have worked years and years fulfilling your purpose, and when you leave these earthly confines you will be able to know your noble purpose is continuing to impact those you love.

As your estate grows begin to save your wealth. Save your profits in liquid assets, paper, and certificates of deposit. Reinvest your profits in liquid investments to cover any cash flow problems. Continue to use OPW, other people's wealth, and find partners and lenders. Make sure you maintain perfect credit, and always pay your bills on time.

Be aware of the difficulty investors have with bankers. An investor is happy with a wholesale purchase of a million-dollar apartment building, which has market value equity of $200,000, using no money down. Unfortunately, most bankers see the deal as a million-dollar liability! Why do bankers have such sour faces when they look at your coup? They use an asset liability ratio on your financial statement, which means they divide your assets by your liabilities. Unless you can provide an acceptable appraisal for your property they will put the asset value of your purchase as the purchase price. Hence, you paid one million dollars and you have a million-dollar note, therefore, to the banker you have no equity, and the million-dollar note is an obligation that the banker has difficulty in understanding why you took it on in the first place! In developing your strategy keep in mind the asset liability ratio. Always upgrade your businesses and properties, and develop your equity position in each business and property. Use options. Options are assets with no liability, which improves your ratio. When you pull profits out of real estate re-invest them in cash flow investments like discounted notes. Then your banker is your friend and your banker will be paying for the lunch. Continue to convert your business activity into liquid assets which are invested at high yields, and maintain your long term equity building assets. Develop and maintain a cash reserve large enough to pay twelve months of payments for operating expenses. Develop credit lines for negative cash flow or use partners to cover any negative cash flow. In real estate, if you have negative cash flow on any of your properties, be sure the property has other benefits which offset the negative cash flow.

Don't forget to pay yourself. Blow some money and some time to reward yourself for your efforts.

Use some of your income for education. Continue to learn a specialty. Become an expert.

Be generous. Give some of your money away to the less fortunate and support your purpose in life. Give to Spiritual organizations, charities and causes you support. These principles work! Read “The richest man in Babylon” by George Clason, and “Think and Grow Rich” by Napoleon Hill.

A word about your partners: Treat your partners’ right. They are the source of greater wealth, inner and outer. It is one of the most satisfying experiences to have lasting business relationships where both partners benefit. Real estate is a long term business and look for long term partnerships. Find partners who will celebrate the good times and peacefully endure the down times and you will end up with some lifelong friends.

"When I let go of what I am, I become what I might be." Lao Tzu

THE FREEDOM MATRIX

When you set up your life to be spectacular and your business to run without you then you will have more free days. Free days are days to do whatever you want to do. Vacation; volunteer, time with your family, you name it. Also, you will have time to work on your purpose, your mission in life. You will have time to express what you are exceptional at. Look at the following matrix. When you know who you are and what your mission in life is, you can apply it to any company or activity or project you can think of.

Personal

[Company 1] [Company 2] [Project 1] [Project 2]

Spiritual

Mental

Physical

Relationships

Organization

Financial

Business

[Company 1] [Company 2] [Project 1] [Project 2]

Your Purpose

Branding

Leadership

Clients for Life

- Relationship Building
- Avatar
- Niche Market
- Lifetime value of a Client
- Follow up
- Marketing

Competition

Partners

Raising Money

Team

Systems

Financial

Legal

Wouldn't it be nice to have a network of individuals who have achieved this? Wouldn't it be nice to have a group to share and be accountable for your journey? Well the group is here at the Matrix Financial Network.

"Happiness is the meaning and the purpose of life, the whole aim and end of human existence." Aristotle

MATRIX FINANCIAL NETWORK

Networking is an important component of success. The synergy in an organization is a network. The attractions in networks are bonds. The bond is a relationship, and relationships are the most important element in networking.

MatrixFinancialNetwork.com is a network of individuals, investors, experts, entrepreneurs who are interested in business, real estate and notes. The site is a network. You can network with the experts you need for your business. These experts can open the doors to larger networks where they are members. The network guides you into relationships which will benefit you. The principles in this book are put into action. You can put your purpose in life into action

Also, *MatrixFinancialNetwork.com* is a mastermind group. There are several kinds of mastermind groups. Earlier in this book we explored the benefits of having an expert mastermind group. This is a group of experts focused on your business and your life. Another type of mastermind group is a group of your peers. When you are a member of this type of mastermind group you benefit from the advice of your peers and you benefit by giving advice to others. This is a safe place to discuss your successes and challenges in business and in life. You can get access to mastermind groups where you can participate and explore your business and life at *MatrixFinancialNetwork.com.*

Go to *MatrixFinancialNetwork.com.*

www.ingramcontent.com/pod-product-compliance
Lightning Source LLC
Chambersburg PA
CBHW072352200326
41519CB00015B/3742
* 9 7 8 0 6 9 2 7 4 0 1 7 0 *